W(HIS)ORSHIP MAJESTY

HOW PRAISING

THE KING OF KINGS WILL

CHANGE YOUR LIFE

JACK W. HAYFORD

Regal

A Division of Gospel Light
Ventura, California, U.S.A.

Published by Regal Books
A Division of Gospel Light
Ventura, California, U.S.A.
Printed in U.S.A.

Regal Books is a ministry of Gospel Light, an evangelical Christian publisher dedicated to serving the local church. We believe God's vision for Gospel Light is to provide church leaders with biblical, user-friendly materials that will help them evangelize, disciple and minister to children, youth and families.

It is our prayer that this Regal book will help you discover biblical truth for your own life and help you meet the needs of others. May God richly bless you.

For a free catalog of resources from Regal Books and Gospel Light, please call your Christian supplier or contact us at 1-800-4-GOSPEL.

Revised and expanded edition. *Worship His Majesty* was originally published by Word Publishing in 1987.

Cover Design by Kevin Keller
Interior Design by Robert Williams
Revised Edition Edited by David Webb

LIBRARY OF CONGRESS CATALOGING-IN-PUBLICATION DATA
Hayford, Jack W.
    Worship His majesty / Jack W. Hayford. — Rev. and expanded ed.
        p.   cm.
    ISBN 0-8307-2398-6
1. God—Worship and love—Biblical teaching.   I. Title.
    BS544 .H39   2000   99-059909
    248.3—dc21

1 2 3 4 5 6 7 8 9 10 11 12 13 14 15 / 05 04 03 02 01 00

Rights for publishing this book in other languages are contracted by Gospel Literature International (GLINT). GLINT also provides technical help for the adaptation, translation and publishing of Bible study resources and books in scores of languages worldwide. For further information, write to GLINT, P. O. Box 4060, Ontario, CA 91761-1003, U.S.A. You may also send e-mail to Glintint@aol.com, or visit the GLINT website at www.glint.org.

CONTENTS

A GOD-SHAPED PLACE

In a tropical rain forest a tribal chieftain bows before a crude figure fashioned from sticks and stones bound together by jungle vines. Somewhere in Asia in a fantastically ornate temple a young man burns incense before a lavishly decorated Buddha. In the heartland of America, a small group of locals meet in an unobtrusive building in a small Nebraska town to sing and pray together. A man in the suburbs of Detroit spends the entire morning meticulously washing and waxing his foreign-made sports sedan, while his teenage daughter spends hours in a poster-plastered room listening to CDs by her favorite rock superstar.

All of these people are worshiping. In some cases the worship follows a prescribed formula within a formalized setting and is relatively easy to identify as worship. Others of these many would generally hesitate to call worship at all. But whether or not we recognize the form it takes, every one of us worships something or someone. And you should understand that whom or what you worship exerts tremendous influence over what you are—and what you will become.

DEFINING WORSHIP

Man is a worshiper by nature. Whether we acknowledge it or not, whether we recognize the object of our affections as a deity in the strict sense of the word or not, we all worship something. Some people worship at the altar of their jobs. Some of us worship money, others their possessions. Some people worship ideals, goals or desires, while others worship pleasure. Some of us even have the audacity to worship God!

Many people don't recognize the fact that they are engaged in the practice of worship because they don't have a clear idea of what worship means. Understanding the meaning of worship is a good beginning place for a book about worship, because until we understand its meaning, we will never understand its exercise.

The word "worship" is derived from the old English *weorth-scipe* and means to ascribe worth unto a being or object. We'll look at this concept more in depth later, but the essential idea is that whatever you value most highly or place the greatest worth upon, that is what you worship. So you can see that people worship many different things, although we can justly say that worship rightfully belongs to God alone, for He is the Creator of all things and all people. No one else but God can truthfully lay claim to the position of highest value in any person's life.

YOU BECOME LIKE THE GOD YOU WORSHIP

Psalm 115:4-8 is one of the most insightful passages on the subject of worship found anywhere in the Bible:

> Their idols are silver and gold,
> The work of men's hands.
> They have mouths, but they do not speak;
> Eyes they have, but they do not see;
> They have ears, but they do not hear;
> Noses they have, but they do not smell;
> They have hands, but they do not handle;
> Feel they have, but they do not walk;
> Nor do they mutter through their throat.
> Those who make them are like them;
> So is everyone who trusts in them.

In this passage, the psalmist describes idolatry and the inadequacy of the false gods worshiped by the heathen. Then he makes a very important observation: Those who make idols are like them, and so is everyone who trusts in them. In other words, you shall become like the god you worship.

Let me say that again because this point cannot be overemphasized: *You become like the god you worship.*

The act of worship means you are developing a set of values; you are determining what you desire most. Worship means you are choosing priorities; you are establishing what comes first in your life. Worship means you are determining what you are to become; you are choosing in whose image you will be made.

Just as God created man and woman in His image, the gods we choose to worship manifest their attributes in the worshiper. So in deciding what or whom to worship, you are making life decisions regarding your values, your priorities and how you are to live.

Your worship will determine what flows from your life. Humankind's highest attainment comes through glorifying God who is worthy of all glory. Some may find temporal glory in their works or pursuits, but that kind of glory fades. Some may even be remembered beyond their lifetimes for achievments in the arts, the sciences or sporting events. But all the accolades, all the medals, all the record books will mean absolutely nothing when we stand before the judgment seat of Christ.

But those who worship the Lord—looking to the unseen rather than to the seen as we go through our present trials—will find what Paul calls an "eternal weight of glory" working in their lives (2 Cor. 4:17). Those will possess a glory that endures.

WHAT DO YOU WORSHIP?

So you can see that some very significant issues are raised by how you worship. Have you determined where you are going to bow? By bowing I don't just mean a physical posture but a stance of the soul. Whom do *you* seek? What do you pursue? To whom or what do you submit? The goal that you press toward—the object of your worship—will be the guiding force of your life.

The one who seeks the Lord will find Him (see Deut. 4:29); he will discover the true purpose for which he was made and, ultimately, will experience the fulfillment of that purpose. He who follows another god will discover what that god provides, whether it is worry, decadence or emptiness.

J. B. Phillips has said there is a God-shaped vacuum in every one of us, a vacuum that only God can fill. Worship is a way to fill that place within us.

Augustine said, "Lord, You've made us for Yourself, and our hearts find no rest till they find it in You." We were created by Him and for Him, and the fulfillment of our hearts' longing comes as a direct result of our approaching Him and coming to know Him. Nothing else can fill that God-shaped place in us— only the Lord Himself.

God reveals Himself to those who bow before Him and seek Him. If you truly seek Him with all your heart, you will find Him. Then when you discover what He's really like, glorifying Him will be the only natural response. Worship will lead you along that path.

MAJESTY

We stood in silent awe, sensing God's presence as shafts of sunlight arrowed through the gracefully arched windows high in the vaulted towers of the vacant abbey. The British countryside was welcoming another summer's morn as we ambled through the partially restored ruins of this ancient house of worship. Although for the most part it was a disheveled and dilapidated site, a dignity remained which was only a trace of the beauty it had known six centuries before at its dedication.

For two weeks my wife, Anna, and I had been probing the corners of Scotland, Wales and England in our tiny rental car, setting our own pace as we drove from place to place. We were slowly becoming accustomed to a left-hand-drive roadway system, but caution and patience were still required. So we chose a leisurely pace, visiting castles and cottages at our whim, no demands dictating our schedule except that we be at Oxford the third week of July. I was to participate in a conference there, studying the phenomenon of spiritual awakenings in a seminar under Dr. Edwin Orr's direction, after which we would return home to Los Angeles.

That summer the whole nation was enjoying a certain regal festivity in anticipation of the silver anniversary of Elizabeth's coronation as queen, and it was amid this prevailing air of rejoicing in royalty that we were introduced to England. Landing in Glasgow, after 10 days of preaching in Denmark, we began our journey—sampling the variety of climates, customs, cuisine and clothing styles from Inverness to Edinburgh to Llangollen to the Cotswolds. By the time we arrived in London, a special sense of wonder had overtaken us.

Occasionally I attempted to put into words the emotions I felt as history spoke to me at every turn. Whether we were quietly sitting in a park, reading an engraved plaque antedating us by centuries, strolling beside the Thames or pushing our way through the crowds shopping at Harrod's, an illusive sense of the *grand*, the *regal* and the *noble* captured my imagination, although eluding my efforts at definition. However, on a side trip we made into Oxfordshire, that definition came by surprise and included a lesson I hadn't expected—and resulted in a song I hadn't sought.

It happened the day we drove to Blenheim.

Blenheim Palace is the massive estate built at Queen Anne's order in the early eighteenth century. She presented it to John Churchill, the first duke of Marlborough, in honor of his leadership in the military victories against Spain. Two centuries later, Winston Churchill would be born and raised here, and during

World War II would frequently retire to this site for rest from the rigors of leadership. It was at Blenheim that many of his stirring speeches were written, speeches that successfully inspired the English people to sustain their efforts at staving off Hitler's Luftwaffe which was close to suffocating their will to survive.

A PERSON OF DESTINY

However, WW II was a full generation past now, and we were walking through the spacious palace which had taken more than 18 years to build. But it was after we passed outside and surveyed the sprawling grounds, so meticulously groomed and magnificently flowered, that the undefined feeling now surfaced and blossomed into a clear, complete thought. While overlooking the palace and grounds from the southwest and contemplating Churchill's former presence on the paths and fields, I mused aloud, "Being raised in such an environment would certainly make it far more credible for a person to conceive of himself as a person of destiny."

The idea effervesced within me. I seemed to have touched the nerve of a concept that had to do with far more than Blenheim and Churchill. It had first to do with that *something* Anna and I had felt these weeks as we traveled around Britain. But it also extended to a fundamental issue of human nature: the grounds for self-worth and the purpose of human existence. All tied in together were unspoken questions and partial answers concerning how people perceive themselves and God's order of things. In some special way there were traces of a larger and more complete pathway to an individual's discovering his true identity and purpose—something realized in an undeclared but real national consciousness.

I'm not presuming that in one instant I plumbed the depths of a nation's psyche. But I did feel that somehow my single observation began to explain a great deal of the spirit that permeates this small nation of such historic consequence. Here only a generation ago an outnumbered band, surpassed by superior technology, withstood the most sinister and vicious manifestation of evil in history to date. Motivating them was an inherent sense of righteousness, but driving the will to hold their ground was an awakened sense of destiny coupled with a historic sense of royalty as a clan.

Even as I stood there, millions of common folk of ordinary means were enthused and excited about celebrating one woman's royal ascent a quarter of a century earlier. This wasn't a case of idolatry, nor was it an instance of the mindless masses cowering before a ruling tyrant with no choice of doing otherwise. On the contrary, the people were rejoicing. The entire kingdom was buoyed by a general mood of personal and national significance. And it seemed inescapably linked in some mystical way to the fact that each person perceived himself to be connected to and personally represented by the one who wears the crown and bears the scepter. Visitors from another country recognize a national dignity that flows to the general citizenry from the regal office of a single individual who reigns over them, exercising authority as an ennobled friend rather than as a feudal overlord.

Then a second thought exploded to consciousness: This is the essence of the relationship Jesus wants us to have with His Church! He wants the fullness of His power, the richness of His nature, the authority of His office and the wealth of His resources to ennoble our identity and determine our destiny!

Notwithstanding the deep emotion filling my soul, a holy calm and genuine joy possessed me. Standing there, my gaze sweeping the scene once again—verdant, lush fields, fragrance of roses everywhere, magnificence in architecture with the stateliness of historic bearing—I gently squeezed Anna's hand.

"Honey, I can hardly describe to you all the things that this setting evokes in me," I said. "There is something of a *majesty* in all this, and I believe it has a great deal to do with why people who lived here have been of such consequence in the shaping of history. I don't mean that buildings and beauty can beget greatness, but I do feel that some people fail to perceive their possibilities because of their dismal surroundings."

As we continued our walk, I spoke further of my concerns with which she agreed. She felt, as I did, a pastoral longing for people to understand the fullness of Jesus, to perceive His high destiny for each of them—to see that our self-realization only comes through a real realization of Him! How completely and unselfishly He invites us to partnership with Him in His Kingdom! How much of His Kingdom authority He wants to transmit to and through us as a flow of His life, love and healing to a hopeless and hurting world!

Now something expanding and deepening that understanding was welling up within me. What had been undefined but sensed for more than two weeks of vacation journeying was now distilling into a single moment of awareness.

Majesty.

The word was crisp in my mind.

Majesty, I thought. It's the quality of Christ's royalty and Kingdom glory that not only displays His excellence but which also lifts us by His sheer grace and power, allowing us to identify with and share in His wonder.

Majesty.

As Queen Elizabeth's throne somehow dignifies every Englishman and makes multitudes of others partakers in a commonwealth of royal heritage, our ascended Savior sits enthroned and offers His regal resources to each of us.

Majesty.

As a nation rose against the personification of evil in the Nazi scourge, ignited to action by a leader who perceived himself a person of destiny, created by a childhood identification with the majestic, so may the Church arise.

Kingdom authority.

"In My name they shall cast out demons," the King declared. And in going forth by the power flowing from His throne, the Lord worked with them, confirming the word with signs following (see Mark 16:17,20).

The crowds were increasing at Blenheim, and the marvel of the moment seemed no less real for becoming less intimate. "Let's go, honey," I said, and we started for the car. My soul was still resonating to the sound of a distant chord struck in heaven but still a lost chord to much of the Church.

WORSHIP HIS MAJESTY

As Anna and I drove along the narrow highway, the road undulating from one breathtaking view to another, I said to her, "Take the notebook and write down some words, will you, Babe?"

I began to dictate the key, the musical notes, the time value of each and the lyrics (and she still insists that *she* wrote the song!):

Majesty, worship His Majesty!
Unto Jesus be all glory, honor and praise.
Majesty, Kingdom authority,
Flows from His throne, unto His own,
His anthem raise.

So exalt, lift up on high the name of Jesus.
Magnify, come glorify, Christ Jesus the King.

Majesty, worship His Majesty.
Jesus who died, now glorified,
King of all kings.

As the event actually happened, I completed neither the lyrics nor the music until weeks later after we returned home. The piece was refined and edited at the piano in our living room, but the song was born in a moment of envisioning the power of the majestic to transform a people and infuse them with a sense of significance and destiny.

At a time in history when more and more people lack this sense of worth, at a time when the Church is uniquely equipped to address that emptiness, this song sounds forth a prophetic message:

Rise, O Church, worship His Majesty!
Your strength is to stand before your King,
For from His throne all power in heaven and earth
    flows unto His own who worship Him.
He who died has ascended.
Exalt Him, for in so doing He will exalt His own
    and make them triumphant in this their hour
    of high destiny and purposed victory!
Worship His Majesty.

The song has begun.
This book elaborates its meaning for all who sing it.

JACK W. HAYFORD
The Church On The Way
The King's Seminary
Van Nuys, California

CHAPTER 1

REFORMATION II

He who has an ear, let him hear what the Spirit says to the churches.

REVELATION 3:6

I propose we drive a nail in the altar.

Or the pulpit.

Or the communion table.

Or the organ bench or pipes.

Or the choirmaster's music stand.

Any place both visible and sufficiently shocking to provide a counterpart to the ancient door at Wittenberg.

When Martin Luther nailed his "Ninety-Five Theses" to the university entryway, the sparks from his hammer ignited the Reformation.

Nearly a half-millennium ago the Church was shaken to its roots, dragged by the nape of the neck to confront the reality of God's Word and forced to face the fact that its forms had chained its people rather than freed them.

The dual truths of "justification by faith" and "the priesthood of the believer" were trumpeted forth and the true Church—the people of God—was released through a recovery of the revelation of God's Word.

We're overdue for another event such as this.

Or are we in the earthquake throes of a new reformation right now but haven't yet defined its epicenter?

I think so. I think the twentieth century was a 100-year travail that has given birth to more than just a Third Millennium. Amid new life being birthed into her by the Holy Spirit, I believe we are about to see The Church Glorious emerge on the world scene!

I do not doubt that Christ could come again today. Whether He does or not, one thing is clear: The Holy Spirit *already has*, and He's moving through the Temple and turning over tables. The surging waves of renewal's tide are flowing deeper and deeper until, now, the only way to escape is to flee to the high tower of traditionalism.

TRYING TO "KEEP CONTROL"

There is an unholy propensity in human nature to secure itself in history rather than open itself to simplicity—the simple touch of God or the summoning voice of the Spirit. Just as in the time of the Reformation, ecclesiastical and theological resistance sustains its posturing against the new, the fresh and the childlike. The effort to "keep control" breeds the forging of new instruments of doctrinaire domination over the Church:

- Simple openness to the Holy Spirit is assaulted as "satanic" because Pentecost's tongues occur again.
- Suggestions that salvation's program intends the reinstatement of human dignity are barraged by accusations of "humanism."
- Distorted applications of God's promises of health and abundance may have been denounced, but any evenhanded attempted to welcome His blessing is also made suspect.
- Proposals that new dimensions of prayer just might turn the day, that social and political transformation are possible through intercession, are deemed presumptuous.
- Proclamation of a bright hope for tomorrow rather than the dismal prospect of defeat and deterioration is said to smack of "seduction."
- Warmth of emotion, expressiveness or spontaneity in worship is challenged as being fanatical, superficial or insincerely casual.

Traditionalism decries these signs of voices "crying in the wilderness," calling for a preparing of the way of the Lord—the way for His Church to move into a new era. Many themes are suggested by the brief observations I've just made, but I am only dealing with one of them in this book.

A REFORMATION IN WORSHIP

I do not propose that this book is the counterpart to Luther's theses, but I would hope that it might become one of 95 (or more) statements—a composite of calls from many quarters contributing to a new Reformation.

I want to underscore that the reformation in worship is in progress. It's already begun, and its fruit has been tested and proven worthy in a sufficient number of situations to show we are not simply dealing with a fad.

I do believe in the vision of The Church Glorious—the here-and-now unveiling of the Bride of Christ in a dimension of purity and power unknown heretofore. I *don't* believe in triumphalism—that pretend world of the religious idealist who supposes a band of supersaints will rise to take the earth by force and dominate society through supernatural power or political control. But there is a *kingdom* to be taken, and there is a *force* to be exerted, and the people of the Highest are the ones to do both.

REDEFINING, UNWRAPPING, UNSEALING

I believe the pathway for the Church's moving into its full destiny in God's counsels, while retaining a practical sanity and spiritual balance on earth's surface, lies in our ability to perceive the true purpose and spiritual dynamic in worship. What has been defined for so long as an hour's exercise on Sunday, packaged by encultured tradition and preserved in doctrinaire posturing, is being *redefined, unwrapped* and *unsealed* today.

Worship is being *redefined* in terms of its form and focus. It isn't that valid traditions must be scorned or discarded but that newness must refill them with meaning. It isn't that the objective adoration of God is being traded off for a shallow subjectivism on the worshiper's part. Rather, simple, fulfilling intimacy is being discovered by more people as they praise Him.

Worship is being *unwrapped* in the removal of sectarian prejudices that have preempted interdenominational participation in biblical practices of worship heretofore labeled and shelved by feuding parties in the Body of Christ. Upraised hands are less and less a badge of the charismatic, instead becoming a simple sign of Christian praise. A learned appreciation for the dignity of liturgical life is increasingly finding a place among people who otherwise would have deemed it lifeless.

Worship is being *unsealed* as well. A theology of worship is coming into perspective that lends biblical dimension to the whole reformation process. The lid of traditional theology is being lifted: Worship is being proposed as a dignifying, empowering act for *man*. And yet God is not being made man's servant.

The historic approach to the doctrine of worship has focused so much on God, in an effort to verify His glory and underscore man's unworthiness, that an unwitting surrender to "works" in worship has resulted. For example, the honest quest to worthily worship God as He deserves to be worshiped easily

WORSHIP HOLDS THE SOLUTION TO THE DILEMMA OF MANKIND.

becomes performance-oriented and hermetically sealed to keep out simple love, warmth and emotion. The intellectual and artistic demands of religious duty may intrude upon the best intent of the worshiper, and suddenly we become those who draw near with their lips but whose hearts are far from God (see Matt. 15:8).

The fruit of the Reformation of Luther, Calvin, Zwingli, Knox and Huss's time was the unchaining of God's people. A new faith, not in Church tradition but in the person of Jesus as the justifying Savior, filled the hearts of millions. With that release—to stand conscience-free before the Judge of the universe and look up into His face and live in His peace—there came a new sense of destiny. The shackles of emotional, intellectual and spiritual slavery were cast aside and a renaissance of learning and social advancement was realized.

I believe a new reformation in worship will accomplish the same thing. This comes at a time when the relevance of the Church is being newly challenged by an intellectually astute and technologically advanced, yet relationally disintegrating and spiritually thirsty, society.

An awakening to the power of worship to reinstate God's divine intent for man can answer contemporary questions as to human purpose. A drug-drunk, suicide-prone, binge-oriented generation lives on that ragged edge because it has become dissipated by its empty affluence of information, experience and pleasure. In the midst of everything, so few have anything; and the questions arise again and again: What are we here for? Why are things as they are?

This is not an exaggeration of the problem with people today, and neither is it an exaggeration to say that worship holds the solution to their dilemma.

THE BITE IN WORSHIP

The reformation breakthrough I propose will require a confrontation with the tidiness of our systems. Just as Luther's voice provoked existing religious structures, so it seems to irritate some today when the neatness of prescribed worship ideas and methods are confronted with fresh approaches and new insights. The "bite" in worship presses in, calling for the sacrifice of everything in us that seeks to secure itself in humanly devised systems of thought and practice. This bite calls us to move from our presuppositions into an honest confrontation with worship's foundational requirement: sacrifice.

Sacrifice has always been involved at the heart of all worship of the Most High; it is the bite in worship. By bite I mean the cost—and the price is usually blood. Blood, that is, as in life—the laying down of what we scream to preserve or spare in our own interest.

With Abel it meant an animal's blood.

With Abraham it meant circumcision.

With Israel it meant the Passover.

With David it meant exuberance.

With Ezra it meant confrontation with opposition.

With Jerusalem's multitudes it meant palms and shoutings.

With Pentecost's participants it meant supernatural praises.

With Paul it meant singing with grace in one's heart.

With Peter it meant a totally new priestly order involving *you*.

In every case there was—there *is*—a bite in worship, a price that confronts the cultural tastes of man. As much as we want beauty and as beautiful as worship may be, with God, beauty is always secondary—life precedes loveliness. He resists whatever obstructs that life, no matter how "beautiful" the human option may appear.

Cain preferred the beauty of the bloodless.

Society mocked the mutilation of Abraham's "mark."

Egypt scorned the bloody doorposts of the Hebrews.

Michal was disgusted with her husband David's dancing to God.

Ezra's spiritual warfare-unto-worship crowds our religious comfort zone.

The Pharisees would have had a more orderly Triumphal Entry—if one at all.

The analysts of Pentecost determined the worshipers were drunk.

Paul's song was reduced to a form rather than released in the Spirit.

Peter's "living stone"-built sanctuary has become petrified in tradition.

Tradition.

We love it and we hate it. We would die for it, but we can't live with it. Its role in worship is pervasive; no part of human experience is more shaped by tradition than the way we worship. Even in the Body of Christ, frequently the force of tradition overrides the truth of God's Word. Whether we like to acknowledge it or not, we prefer worship styles that suit taste and tradition *first,* and the truth is often quite secondary where worship's demand, or bite, is concerned.

Discerning between the principles of worship and the practice of worship is the demanding challenge we face. And to do so is to risk discarding our security blanket of "warm fuzzy" feelings about worship and to press for the fashioning of a new wardrobe of priestly garments. As with any wardrobe, we need a pattern to follow.

A PATTERN OF PURSUIT

"To Him who loved us and washed us from our sins in His own blood, and has made us kings and priests to His God" (Rev.

1:5,6). These words supply a pattern for our quest of reformed and refined worship.

First, this pattern exalts the *person* we worship: Jesus, who died to redeem us from the sin curse of eternal death and who did so at the expense of His own lifeblood shed on the Cross.

Second, it qualifies the *practice* of our worship: a priestly ministry, prioritized by this designation to remind us that worship involves the priestly traits of duty and purity. We do well to heed the lessons of Israel's priesthood: Having been "made" priests unto our God and Savior, we have a lifelong call (one never outgrows worship) and a holy calling (purity and piety are not options).

Third, this pattern presents the *perspective* on worship: kingship!

In one verse, we are shown how He who has washed us from our sins and made us priests unto God has also accomplished yet a third miraculous transformation: He has made us kings under the King of kings. Most literally, the text describes us as a kingdom of priests, or to use Peter's words, "a royal priesthood" (1 Pet. 2:9). But the majestic imagery of courts and kingdoms, of regal pomp and circumstance, is used of us nonetheless. Though it may fit few of us from *our* viewpoint of ourselves, still this fundamental thread of thought portraying royal imagery must be dealt with. It's at the heart of grasping His Majesty's call to worship Him as priests and as kings. Kings have to do with ruling, with kingdoms, with authority and, very often, with warfare. Too seldom has worship been seen as related to spiritual warfare and conquest. But worship is intended to introduce God's kingdom-power *throughout* the Church and to extend that power *through* the Church.

Kingdom authority is the issue.

The worship of Christ should show itself in more than aesthetic brilliance or doctrinal excellence. It is intended to distill the authority of Jesus among and upon the lives of the worshipers, to infuse their lives so that it might influence everything *they* influence.

The bottom line is *Kingdom authority*.

Majesty, worship His Majesty!
Unto Jesus be all glory, honor and praise.
Majesty, Kingdom authority,
Flows from His throne, unto His own,
His anthem raise.

It is the Reformation perspective of this hymn that *all* praise and worship are due to God's Son, who alone is the Lord of our salvation and the one mediator between God and man. But it is also the "Reformation II" perspective of this hymn that God's worship plan ushers in a present release of His power—an operational dimension of His love and life—in the midst of all who worship Him in spirit and truth.

A reformation in worship will apply its bite. Reformations do that—pressing against any resistance of human pride and pushing us past any personal preoccupation with our "warm fuzzies."

CHAPTER 2

IT WAS MEANT TO BE SO DIFFERENT

Every valley shall be exalted and every mountain and hill brought low . . .
[and] the glory of the Lord shall be revealed, and all flesh shall see it together.

ISAIAH 40:4

Richard and Michelle's baby died.

It was a case of crib death—that unexplained, invisible suffo-cator of infants. Besides being devoted parents, Richard and Michelle were also faithful servants to the congregation to whom they ministered as pastoral assistants. Now as news spread of the baby's tragic death and as people in the church searched for answers, a clutter of questions was buzzing overhead like a swarm of flies:

"Where is God when things like this are happening?"

"They're such a sweet couple. What did they do to deserve this?"

"Why does God allow these things? After all, the little thing was so helpless."

"She was such a sweet baby. How will they handle the pain?"

But Richard and Michelle didn't have any questions.

Only tears.

Grief was deeply and understandably present, but so was a warm, very human and unpretentious simplicity of faith. They knew Kirstin's death had nothing to do with God; He neither willed her death nor took her life, nor did He watch the passing of their child with indifference.

Within their sorrow and undiluted by their tears, a quiet confidence reigned—a kind of rule which prevails when people understand that such situations are neither God's will nor God's fault, that tough things happen because our planet is sadly out of joint with God's intended order of things. They knew the facts that pertain to humankind's forfeited rulership of a world entrusted to them by the Creator, and understood the problems of living in a world now "on its own" by man's own willful choice. They knew the truth that people have become painfully vulnerable to the consequences of a lost government—a maverick unpredictability now prevailing all too often. They knew that in His original design God meant everything to be quite different.

Richard and Michelle discovered these truths in learning to worship.

Through years of preparation for ministry they had grown in Christ and in understanding. And they had grown in a pattern of giving and serving in Jesus' name. Their baby's death staggered them, but they didn't stumble, instead exhibiting a steadfastness that was neither feigned nor forced. They had a solid perspective on "man as he was meant to be."

The role of worship in their lives was foundational and essential to their stability, for at its core, worship is not a kind of church service so much as an understanding of life—how to rule in life rather than being ruled by it—even when tragedy strikes.

THE PRIMAL TRAGEDY

Most people who know the Bible perceive that the presence of all adversity in our world dates to the primal tragedy: the fall of man from his first estate in creation's order. The opening pages of Scripture succinctly set the stage for our understanding of God's love-plan of recovery for our race. God's Word describes the reason for the human dilemma. The biblical record of (1) creation's perfect and original order, (2) man's intended destiny and (3) the fouling of them both does more than merely place blame. This record of failure also introduces hope.

And it establishes the foundation of purpose and promise for our lives by introducing us to worship. At the root of God's revelation to His creation, worship is shown as the prerequisite for man's ability to receive and live within the high possibilities and rich benediction of God's plan.

Yet even though the opening chapters of Genesis set forth worship as the foundation for building a successful life, until a few years ago, I had never before seen this truth. I trace my blindness to this perspective to an inadequate explanation I had been given for man's creation: the widely quoted and generally accepted half-truth that "God created man for fellowship."

That statement is so often glibly repeated by Christians that one might think it was in the Bible. Yet it's only a fraction of the whole truth and it's drastically less than what the Creator had in mind when He created man.

Of course fellowship with God is a rich part of the privilege granted to humans. But there is something of an underlying shallowness to the proposition that fellowship was God's sole or primary purpose in making us. It somehow presents the picture of a lonesome deity who conjures up creatures to ensure He will have friends present at His weekend parties. The Bible teaches differently.

God's own Word clearly reveals that He was creating people not so much for fellowship as He was establishing them for *rulership*—granting us a relationship with our Creator that would give us the ability to carry out our intended role on earth: to become rulers.

Created for Rulership

When the Three-in-One determined to "make man in Our image," a reason was given: "Let them [humankind] have dominion" (Gen. 1:26,28). God's purpose for creating man and woman, while including fellowship, was definitely much more. God was inviting us into *partnership* with Him. We were being made kings, and our dominion was to be all the earth.

The dimensions of God's domain and ours were vastly different. God was and is Creator and Ruler of the entire universe, while we were created to be rulers over one planet (see Ps. 115:16). But there is no escaping one awesome fact: Without jealousy for His own power and at great risk and potential cost to Himself, God not only created a being with certain capacities much like His own, but He also welcomed that creature into a kind of co-regency—at least insofar as Earth was concerned. The privilege of rulership was our assigned role, but resource for its performance was dependent upon a foundational relationship: Our rule was to be sustained by our worship of Him. The creator-creature relationship made worship appropriate, and our finite resources mandated it. So it was at the beginning; so it is today.

He who wakened to his being in the garden looked into the face of the One who had breathed existence into him, and he knew beyond question the source of his life. Thanksgiving for his being initiated man's worship.

He stood upright as no other creature and gazed beyond the horizon of his earth-home to behold the stars, and he intuitively knew the heavens were the handiwork of the One who had formed his physical frame. Humility and awe at the Creator's power were added worship themes amid the garden.

He who received the first commandments—be fruitful, multiply, replenish the earth, subdue it and exercise dominion—was sensitized to the reality that awesome powers had been entrusted to him. Acknowledged dependency was the only possible response to the magnanimity of a Creator who shared such power with His creation.

He who heard the sole restriction incumbent upon him—"Of the tree of the knowledge of good and evil you shall not eat" (Gen. 2:17)—perceived his finiteness and his accountability to One wielding infinitely higher authority than he. Knowing that true worship requires the conclusive and ultimate response of obedience, man the worshiper obeyed.

For how long man walked with God in this relationship—a relationship founded on worship and daily responding with thanksgiving, humility, awe, dependency and obedience—we have no knowledge. But there was an unblemished era of obedience when man the worshiper of God partnered with the

Almighty as man the ruler. He tasted the delight of complete fulfillment, broad authority, wide possessions and personal significance. Within the circle of a relationship that released his highest potential, he also enjoyed a companion-like fellowship with
the Almighty One, his maker.

And then man fell.

The one condition on which rested the joy derived from his
relationship and his rulership was violated. When Adam dis-
obeyed, he severed the bond of obedient worship. He no longer
worshiped in the spirit of thanks, humility, awe and dependency. His relationship with the Creator was broken. His pristine
dignity was lost and his authority for rulership surrendered.
Because the damning act had been the result of obeying the serpent's lie, he had both yielded his trust and forfeited his rule to
the tempter of mankind.

This double tragedy—the loss of man's rule under God and
its placement into the gnarled claws of the dragon—constitutes
the basic explanation for the deadly, the destructive and the
damning acts that daily wreak havoc upon our world.[1]

At this point in the narrative, what was lost through the
violation of worship's proper order seems hopelessly gone. But
God's Word immediately introduces hope: The Creator is
about to disclose a plan by which man's intended purpose in
His will can be regained. This plan will involve the reinstatement of man and woman through the reestablishment of pure
worship.

BEGINNING REINSTATEMENT

The wonder of God's infinite wisdom lies not so much in His
power to create as in His power to redeem.

Genesis 3 is at once the foundation of man's horror and the fountainhead of his hope. God's love and wisdom shine forth in the speed with which He confronts the disaster sin has introduced to the human race. He immediately sets forward a promise and a provision for mankind's redemption. Only divine wisdom can move so quickly, cover so thoroughly, deal so consistently and love so graciously.

In launching a program of forgiveness and redemption, nothing of His foundational order is violated. With one stroke, God deals with man's fall. In both justice and mercy He confronts the sin and administers specific judgment on each party involved and then turns to solve the long-range need of the lost pair.

We see in this passage a holy determination that all God intended *shall* be recovered. The Father insists that man's destiny shall not be destroyed by hell's plot. An eventual conclusive blow shall be struck—a Redeemer-Seed will be born who will break the power Satan has seized (see Gen. 3:15). And with this promise He unfolds a provision for the two who stand before Him, ashamed, bereft of former glory, severed from God and stripped of the ruling power He had given them.

While the brevity of the Genesis record does not relate the conversation which followed, let us not make the mistake of supposing too much or too little from the text:

> Also for Adam and his wife the LORD God made tunics of skin, and clothed them (Gen. 3:21).

Few words report the provision made for clothing the couple and I'll not suggest that an elaborate outline of redemption's plan was given. But we do know one thing: They understood that the offering of a sacrifice was more than a means for clothing; it instituted the path of worship by which their recovery would be realized.

The evidence of their understanding is confirmed in the following chapter. Fallen man had been given understanding as to the significance and substance of his worship, his offerings to God. That is why Abel obediently practices the worship that had been taught to him by his parents. That is why Cain—fully aware of what God expects in worship and fully warned not to violate the pattern he also had learned—is judged so sharply (see Gen. 4:1-7). The issue is crucial and is also clear: Worship was the foundation of man's being and potential. Thus God's redemptive program is founded in worship.

There is an impressive symmetry in this. Man's relationship and rule under God had been rooted and sustained in worship. Now, just when both seem to be irretrievably lost, God sets forth a recovery plan. With unsurprising consistency, yet with an amazing simplicity, this plan also centers on worship!

POWER
FLOWS FROM
WORSHIP.

There is no show of power.

No display of cosmic almightiness.

No instant smashing of the serpent.

No fury leveled at the guilty.

Instead there is an introduction to a humble act of worship. The Redeemer's grace seems to exceed even His power as He sets forth to recover for His beloved creatures all that has been lost. Yet the program is not as one might expect, for its hidden power is in the reinstatement of worship rather than in a demonstration of might.

The mightiness will flow from worship.

LOST AND RESTORED

Obedience would have been better than sacrifice; but what disobedience lost, sacrifice is going to restore!

The slain animal whose skin provided clothing for the glory-stripped couple forecasts how the coming of the Seed would vanquish the snake. For the promise just given was that moment being fulfilled in part. What the serpent had done in breaching the relationship between man and his Creator, God was undoing with the sacrificial provision—His forecast of an ultimate annulment of the evil power which had intruded into the divine order.

Turning several hundred pages to the Gospel accounts, we leap through the centuries to where we see so clearly the amazing consistency in God's order. The same issue is present in the wilderness as in the garden. When the Seed and the snake have their first head-to-head encounter, the issue is still relationship and rulership. Worship is the summons and nothing less than world rule is at stake.

Again, the devil took Him up on an exceedingly high mountain, and showed Him all the kingdoms of the world and their glory. And he said to Him, "All these things I will give You if You will fall down and worship me." Then Jesus said to him, "Away with you, Satan! For it is written, 'You shall worship the Lord your God, and Him only you shall serve'" (Matt. 4:8-10).

This precise symmetry is foundationally important to our whole understanding. Worship will only make *complete* sense when we understand its place in God's *complete* plan. He did not give worship as a test of wills but as the source of our potential. He has not created man as a pawn or a plaything but to become a partner in His highest purposes.

Just as defiled worship broke man's relationship and forfeited his dominion, restored worship is intended to redeem both relationship and rulership. God's forgiveness of our sin establishes relationship, and His reinstating our intended purpose promises the rulership.

Mankind is being offered both deliverance from evil and dominion over it—a continual walk with God and growing triumph over hell. As in the beginning when the foundations for man's life—his purpose and fulfillment—were laid in worship, so redemption's program seeks to reinstate man by restoring those foundations.

Though man's foundation's were crumbled by his fall, Jesus Himself has established a new beginning point for perfect worship. He is the sacrifice. He is the high priest. He is the leader in worship, restoring any member of Adam's race who will return to relationship with God. But restored relationship through reestablished worship is not the sum of the redemption plan. The full scope of the divine program of retrieval must not be narrowed.

Man's restored relationship with God is intended to restore his rulership as well: "Repent, for the kingdom of heaven is at hand" (Matt. 4:17). Repentance is in essence the renewal of worship. Because repentance resubmits us to God's rule, two lost possibilities reappear: the resurrection of our relationship *with* Him and the restoration of our rulership *under* Him. Our return to our intended place of obedient worship not only places us under God's kingdom rule again; but it thereby also makes possible a reinvestment of that rule among humankind.

Our full understanding of worship's intended potential for our lives is diluted if we miss this point. Just as relationship was not the sole purpose of our creation, so our recovery is not the sole purpose of our salvation. We were also created for rulership, and full salvation includes the restoration of that rule—dominion, authority, creative responsibility and accountability.

Although the fullest implications of our restored rule will not unfold until our eternal future, believers are called *now* "to reign in life" (Rom. 5:17)—to begin relearning the dimensions and the exercise of the dominion first granted to us. In our present lifetime, growth in this plan begins and extends as we learn that worship is the way to all rulership being exercised and all dominion being expanded.

WHAT RULE? WHAT DOMINION?

What are the implications of restored rule, of renewed dominion? The words seem so towering, so potentially high-and-mighty. But the issues are intensely practical and related to the basics of everyday living. And this is important, because it is exactly there that so many believers who have relationship with God seem to fall short in regaining rulership.

Perhaps by looking at what was lost through sin, we might better understand what we can regain:

1. *Man lost his righteous relationship with God*—evidenced by his awareness of his nakedness and his flight from God's presence (see Gen. 3:7-11).
2. *Man lost his healthy relationship with his spouse*—evidenced by accusation and alienation between them and later by family strife between their children (see Gen. 3:12,16,20; 4:8).
3. *Man lost his ability to deal effectively with his environment*—evidenced by the fact that his "workplace" came under a curse, reducing yield and thereby his relative success (see Gen. 3:17-19).
4. *Man lost the promise of life*—evidenced by the entry of disease, depression and death and, apart from redemption, eternal destruction (see Gen. 2:17; 3:19).

To summarize, man lost (1) confidence in his relationship with God, (2) the ability to rule well in his own household, (3) his fruitfulness and effectiveness in his vocation and (4) his certainty of hope for a life characterized by physical, mental and emotional health.

As we consider the enormity of this loss, the Word of God opens the way to an understanding of the practical dimension of dominion we can expect to regain through worship:

1. *Dominion over condemnation.* Worship opens the heart to perceive God's love and grace in a growing way. My

full acceptance in Christ's righteousness establishes a foundation of confidence for living.

2. *Domestic order.* Husband-wife and parent-child relationships begin to change for the better in homes where a spirit of praise and the simple, loving worship of God prevail.

3. *Economic freedom.* A person's ability to succeed in work and advance in his financial situation is verifiable time and again where the principles of worship-with-finance are applied (i.e., stewardship and giving).

4. *Personal wellness.* The praiseful person is destined to be healthier than the cynic simply because the systems of the human body respond positively to a prevailing mental and emotional attitude.

What was lost through defiled worship, God's program of revived worship in Christ can restore! This is what a growing number of people are discovering today.

As the Church experiences a revival in worship, a renewed sense of God's rule is coming into our lives. It's a biblical principle: Where God finds people who will worship within His will, He extends His Kingdom rule through them:

> For the eyes of the LORD run to and fro throughout the whole earth, to show Himself strong on behalf of those whose heart is loyal to Him (2 Chron. 16:9).

Admittedly, a delicate balance must be maintained here.

We can be assured of some restoration of all that was lost in the Fall, but God's Word gives us no guarantee of perfection in any respect until the complete restoration of *all* things in His future Kingdom.

There is a presence of His Kingdom authority bequeathed to His own now, however. Let none of us forfeit the present dimensions of Kingdom authority by not pursuing the recovery of His rulership in our lives. We must not fear beginning that pursuit simply because we feel disqualified by our past failures or by a present sense of weakness. Rulership is a promise; it isn't a presumptuous thing for a saved sinner to expect.

But how do we begin that pursuit?

We shouldn't be surprised to find that worship is the key at every point! As we walk in the Holy Spirit-power of worship, life as God meant it to be *can* be recovered. We can receive all the fullness salvation holds for us as we rebuild the foundations of worship that God first gave to man. "When we keep looking at Jesus with a real openness to the Holy Spirit's ministry, we will begin to brightly reflect the beauty of Christ and keep becoming like Him" (2 Cor. 3:18, author's paraphrase).

Worship recovers all that Adam lost. It is God's way for each of us to find a progressively restored dominion in our lives.

There is no dimension of Adam's loss that may not be recovered now in Christ. Even the dimension of death changes.

First, the hope of eternal life is promised to us, certified with hard evidence—the resurrection of our Lord Jesus Christ! But we all still have an appointment with death (see Heb. 9:27). Not even restored worship can recover immortality this side of heaven. And contrary to the opinion of a few sincere souls, no one can commandeer a certain date or ensure a certain life span.

But whenever death does touch us through the passing of one we love, the spirit of understanding in worship can transform the moment. Though tears may fill our eyes, dominion has returned to our souls. The true worshiper is not ruled by death, neither by its force nor its fear. He has dominion over it.

Ruling in Life

And so that dominion prevailed with Richard and Michelle when baby Kirstin died. Two days after the baby died, with her pastor's wife, Becki, standing by her side, Michelle was looking at the small body in the tiny casket. The bereaved mother smiled slightly.

In a quiet yet strong voice, she spoke: "You know, Kirstin, I thought you were going to be with me all my life. I thought we'd bake cookies together. And I thought you would wear my wedding dress. But you were only going to be here a short time, and I didn't know that."

Then Michelle turned to the woman beside her. Becki's arms had slipped around Michelle's waist, her eyes filling with the tears of a mother who understands, and Michelle said, "Becki, I really only have one thing to say: It's been worth it all. Kirstin has brought Richard and me so much joy in the short time we had her, I cannot be anything but thankful."

She paused. "And you know what, Becki? I can hardly wait to get pregnant again."

* * * * *

Worship is for people—people of Adam's race, whom Jesus Christ is teaching to recover the lost dominion God meant for us all to have. Things may not always be as God intended. Before the foundations crumbled under sin's destructive blow, life was meant to be so different. But just as worship could have preserved man's foundation for dominion, worship can restore whatever dimensions anyone wants to learn and rebuild.

Richard and Michelle learned well.

The question we face together—looking at worship's intended possibilities for restoring man's created role of ruler—is whether we're ready for the new Reformation unto which it calls.

CHAPTER 3

WORSHIP IS FOR PEOPLE

But John's father told him the Steward would be angry if he did not sit
absolutely still and be very good; and John was beginning to be afraid,
as he sat in the high chair with his feet dangling, and his clothes itching
all over him, and his eyes starting out of his head.

C. S. LEWIS, *THE PILGRIM'S REGRESS*

I wasn't yet tuned in to a worship reformation or to the concept
of worship as a means for releasing rulership. I was, however,
ready to challenge the "warm fuzzies" of my own worship tradition, and though I didn't know it, a phenomenal development in
my understanding of worship was about to take place.

It all began with a conversation in an elevator.

The academic dean of the college was asking me to teach a course very unacademically and uncleverly named "Song Direction." I didn't like the idea. In fact, I didn't like anything about the course as it was structured. It seemed to approach church worship services as perfunctory duty and church platform leaders as keepers of the machinery of worship.

"Why do you want me to teach it?" I complained. "I really don't want to. There are lots of other faculty who can handle it at least as well as I could."

"That's just the problem, Jack. No, there aren't."

I was flattered, at least until the dean continued, "Virtually no one else's fall schedule can accommodate the time frame opened for the class, and yours does. Besides, you have a natural gift for music and—well, you're a composer as well, and . . ."

I don't know exactly how the sentence ended. I was busy trying to overcome the scuttling of my flattered feelings, now realizing that my primary qualification for being selected for this assignment was simply my schedule. But the minor lacerations to my pride had been salved somewhat by the allusion to my limited musical skills; and when the new semester opened, I was on the spot.

I had accepted the assignment on the terms that I would be allowed to restructure the course. The dean had approved my syllabus, and we changed the name to "Introduction to Worship."

This was a required class, so the sophomore students were trapped. As they filed in that first day, I could see that their conversations with experienced upperclassmen had not filled them with happy expectations. But as the course progressed and we began to take a fresh look at worship, the dread turned into excitement.

The basis of our examination of worship could be expressed in one basic question: What are church services supposed to be about?

That question spawned a seemingly endless series of others, such as:

Why do we sing in church?

Why are "services" called that?

What are the scriptural grounds for the actions and activities our services comprise?

What is "liturgy"? Do only liturgical churches have liturgies or do we all?

What practices do we observe that have become mere formalism or dead habit? Why are they like that and how did they get that way?

However, as we questioned various worship practices, I cautioned the students to resist an attitude of judgmental criticism or smug snobbishness. "After all," I said, "it is worship we're assessing, so let's operate from this premise: Any wearying habit or dead tradition that we note in our churches was probably good at the start."

That approach did wonders, and I still recommend it to people seeking renewal in their church traditions. When any of us searches for the valid reasons that may have been behind our traditions at their inception, a humble, seeking heart and sympathetic spirit of hunger for truth must be preserved. A prayerful attitude will contribute toward the refreshing we want.

And so as a class we set out to find what generated common "spiritual life forms," when and how they were born and what biblical grounds supported those various practices.

A REFOCUSED VIEWPOINT

The result of this approach was successful, academically speaking; but beyond that, our quest proved to be experientially rejuvenating. Something started vibrating in the class as the students began to tune in to a real spirit of revival. This was much more than I had hoped for, and even the song-leading drill began to throb with life. We had gone beyond analysis to application, for in sensitively discussing what a service was supposed to be, we gained a perspective on a two-edged truth we all had sensed but never before defined:

> A worship service is convened (1) to serve God with our praise and (2) to serve people's need with His sufficiency.

There weren't any new ideas there, but that one sentence served to refocus my idea of worship.

My approach had been primarily oriented toward a single purpose in church services: We gather to worship God. But now, without supplanting the worship of God, we were adding a second focus: man's need and God's ability to supply it.

We had deduced that worship is to be *to* God and *for* man. For me, that simple statement brought new insight into the classic definition of human purpose so frequently quoted from the Westminster Shorter Catechism (1647): "Man's chief end is to glorify God and to enjoy him forever."

I was surprised. The dual emphasis had been there all the time, but I hadn't seen it. The catechism's words had always seemed to strike my ear as exalted and high-sounding. While "to glorify God" is obviously a worthy endeavor, all the sum of the "to enjoy Him forever" seemed distant, reserved for our heavenly future.

But suddenly, to my delight, I saw this classically approved and theologically acceptable statement declaring the same dual truth we were learning about in regard to worship. First, God is to be the focus of our praise; second, He had always planned that in worship we would find joy, blessing, fulfillment and purpose.

There was a simple but fresh touch of life in this discovery.

Indeed, worship is for people, we had concluded, but there were two tests we needed to apply to our discovery: The first had to do with human response, the second with biblical truth.

First, I proposed we examine the elements that most of our worship services comprised. If worship is for people and if God meant worship to restore us, then why are so many people more often bored than blessed? What must we do to reverse our viewpoint from worship as *requirement* to worship as *opportunity*? We went back to the basics.

I was convinced that the practices of worship were designed to fulfill people, and I wanted to overcome any attitude that might diminish that potential for joy. So we turned to Scripture and reviewed these worship mandates:

"ASSEMBLE YOURSELVES TOGETHER" (HEB. 10:25)

Could it be that God calls people together to worship Him and not to cause inconvenience? Could it be that He calls us together, not because worship can't be done in private, but because we are created with so much potential for fulfillment when we come together in the spirit of His love? On the contrary, however, if our gathering is merely by constraint, motivated by guilt or packaged for the institution rather than for the individual, then worship will soon dissolve into drudgery—or slavery.

Many people excuse themselves from their accountability to worship by saying, "I worship God all the time, in whatever I'm doing." That's good. We should allow everything we do to be glorifying to Him. But we also have a need for regular times of concentrated worship with our fellow believers. We need to experience the refreshing at the soul level that comes from worship and fellowship. Hebrews 10:25 tells us this will become all the more important as we see the day of His glorious return approaching—the day we shall be *forever* together.

"SING UNTO THE LORD" (PS. 96:1)

There are 85 places in the Bible where we are directed to sing. Could it be that God calls people to sing their worship to Him, not because He's intent on increasing their cultural awareness or developing their musical skills, but because singing is a natural expression of human joy and love? On the contrary, however, if song is removed from declaring present insights, testimonies and exaltation in God's goodness, it will become less than rejoicing and soon stodginess or dreariness will take over.

God's Word repeatedly and directly tells us that singing releases joy. It's easy to sing when the joy of the Lord fills our hearts, but the Bible says to do it at other times, too. Studying the Psalms, we see David singing to the Lord in the middle of some very difficult situations. And the song he sings isn't always "He has put a new song in my mouth—Praise to our God" (Ps. 40:3). Some of David's songs say, "There are people after me, God! Protect me! Be my shield" (see Ps. 7, for example). In other psalms he expresses confession or sorrow.

As we look at the biblical exhortations to sing, it becomes clear that it is from more than a subjective point of excitement that we sing. Singing is something the Lord has said to do because there is power that is released through song. Even when we don't feel like it, even when it may not be all that exciting at a particular juncture in our lives given the circumstances, to lift our voices to praise Him and worship Him with song exhibits wisdom.

"CONTINUING IN PRAYER, SHARING AND THE APOSTLES' DOCTRINE" (ACTS 2:42)

Here is a cluster of three worship-time practices, each of which allows for the prospect that God meant our time of worship to fulfill us even as we worship Him. Each opens the way to divine possibilities for our lives:

Prayer

The language of worship is found in prayer. Psalm 65:2 says, "O You who hear prayer, to You all flesh will come."

The Lord does hear prayer, and our prayers are offered in many different ways. Yet all prayer is filled with worship in this respect: As we pray we are brought into submission to Him. The Lord's Prayer concludes, "For Yours is the kingdom and the power and the glory forever. Amen" (Matt. 6:13). That's the worship summary statement concerning our prayers: Everything belongs to Him. Let's look at a few different aspects of prayer and how they bespeak the language of worship:

Confession. Although perhaps we haven't recently indulged in gross sin, we need to come simply before God each day and say, "Lord, I'm growing in Your ways, but I'm not there yet. Forgive my shortcomings and continue to shape me into Your image."

Petition. We all face needs for help, provision, strength, healing and wisdom. But we may also inquire, "Lord, what would You have me do? How would You have me arrange the details of my life? I submit them to You and in all my ways acknowledge You, that You may direct my paths."

Praise. Psalm 100:4 says we are to "enter into His gates with thanksgiving, and into His courts with praise." Offering praise to the Lord is not only a means of accessing His throne but is also an appropriate way to remember His goodness every day. Then stepping into His presence, we wait there to receive direction from our living God.

Meditation. This is not some transcendental trip or a superstitious, mystical exercise. Meditation in its purest form means to think upon what the Lord has said and then to wait upon Him, anticipating that He will speak to me through His Word and by His Spirit.

Intercession. It is the great privilege—and responsibility—of believers to contract with the Almighty for the invasion of His force and His might into any situation where the press of circumstance or judgment or the attack of the enemy is coming down on people. For example, 1 Timothy 2:2 directs us to pray for our governmental leaders and all who are in authority "that we may lead a quiet and peaceable life in all godliness and reverence."

Adoration. We are commanded to exalt Him and to adore Him who is worthy. Psalm 99:5 says, "Exalt the Lord our God, and worship at His footstool—He is holy."

The language of worship is sensible. Prayer is man glorifying the living God and, in these ways, we come appropriately before His throne in a sane, sensible and responsible exercise of worship. As we do so, the prayer dimension in worship speaks to us as we speak to Him. God is saying, "I've given this to you as a gift. Worship is for you, as well as for Me."

Preaching

So it is with preaching. Our worship services include a time for the opening of His Word—a time designed to inspire and uplift, to stir faith and to beget hope. Preaching that only informs without inspiring or that only confronts without instilling hope may be orthodox, but it may also be counterproductive.

Long ago Jesus, just prior to His ascension, met with the Twelve as they gathered in Galilee. There they worshiped Him and it was in that atmosphere of worship that He taught them, saying, "All authority has been given to Me in heaven and on earth. [Now] go" (Matt. 28:18,19). To this day, when the Church comes together to worship Him and to hear the Word, we receive the flow of His authority and His commission to go and share Jesus Christ with every person, transforming our world with His power.

As we center our worship on the Word, we are in effect saying to Him, "We honor Your truth, Your revealed will and Your commands." But make no mistake, He is saying in return, "Those who honor My Word will be blessed. Those who receive My promises shall know My highest and best!" (see Isa. 58:13,14).

Yes, worship is unto God, but it is also a gift He has given to us. This is equally true of the third feature of our worship.

Presenting Our Offerings

Here we see man's call to open his heart and his hand. Giving in church should not be seen as a supportive device for God's program, as though our funds will keep His divine plans from teetering over the precarious edge of impending failure until the end of the month. Giving is a plan a loving Father has provided to release His children from selfishness and to allow our entry into His covenant of material blessings.

True, at the heart of the offering of worship is the offering of my life. Yet Paul's words to the Corinthians note a dual dimension: "He who sows sparingly will also reap sparingly, and he who sows bountifully will also reap bountifully" (2 Cor. 9:6).

Paul knew that giving was a spiritual dynamic built into the very fabric of life. When we give our offerings of worship, we give a part of our lives. When we give money, we give a part of our lives. The finances of nearly every home represent an exchange someone received for an investment of his or her time and talents. Worship says, "Lord, You are my life. You have made me what I am and given me the talents to do the work by which You provide for me. Because You've been so faithful to me, I now offer back to You a token of what You have given me." In offering to God what He has given us, we open ourselves to a further flow of His resources and we acknowledge that all of our life originates in Him.

But in the wake of our sowing with worshipful, obedient giving of offerings, God declares, "Now you are going to reap!" as though it were a delight to Him to call us to worship in multiple ways so that He might respond with multiplied blessings.

ANTHROPO-*WHAT?!*

Yes, God has designed worship to be fulfilling to man. But there is a monstrous theological fly in this ointment of prospective joy: *anthropocentrism.* Anthropocentric means to be centered in man. It's a term brandished like a dagger by any theologian who is nervous about experience-oriented spirituality—an anathema pronounced upon anything perceived as making too much of man. Anthropocentrism is considered the unpardonable sin in some quarters of evangelical orthodoxy.

On the one hand such warnings are needed. We need to steer clear of humanistic systems that deify man and reduce God to a parlor pet, making Him something slightly grander than trees and flowers. In that sense, anthropocentrism describes the mind-set of shallow pop theologies birthed in every generation—systems that satisfy man's desire to acknowledge God yet still pursue his own indulgences. Warnings against any deification of humankind are indeed words of wisdom.

But "man-centered" is also a buzzword that is often shouted by clerics at the hint of anything remotely human happening in our churches: people being "blessed," for example, or holiness becoming too "happy." There are some theological purists who feel called to relentlessly defend God's honor, even if their defense is leveled against some of His own people who not only simply love Him but who also love Him simply. Thus, it seems predictable that any challenge to a proposition that worship is required by God to be "solely *unto* Him and *for* Him" might invite charges of man-centeredness.

But just as the validity of the proposition "worship is for people" is shown by the natural joy its exercise generates, so the Bible demonstrates its soundness. True worship is a gift that blesses rather than a chore that we wearily fulfill.

TRUE WORSHIP IS A GIFT THAT BLESSES RATHER THAN A CHORE THAT WE WEARILY FULFILL.

A Bible-centered approach to worship clearly reveals that worship is definitely *not* a God-ordained device to compel man to stroke a heavenly ego. Neither is it a summons to a weekly reaffirmation of one's expertise in precision-cut declarations of doctrinaire posturing. Instead, the Scriptures consistently show God calling His people to worship in His presence so that He might release, redeem, renew and restore them.

> *Item:* God respected and rewarded Abel because his worship acknowledged the one path by which man received God's loving coverage for his sin. His blood sacrifice was based on gratitude for the redemption plan initiated in the Garden, and his worship forecast an expectation of an even greater expression of love—a coming Redeemer. Cain was rejected, not so much for his violation of a religious formula as for the smallness of his jealous heart that failed to grasp the largeness of God's (see Gen. 4:4-7).

> *Item:* Israel was called forth from Egypt "that they may serve Me" (Exod. 8:1). God's plan that they serve Him was not a relocation of slave labor from Egypt's bricks to Sinai's rituals. God delivered His people out of bondage into worship—because through worshiping Him, they would come to know the heart and nature of the One who promised, "I will bring you . . . to a land flowing with milk and honey" (Exod. 3: 17).

> *Item:* One of Jesus' most profound statements about worship was spoken to an immoral woman: "But the hour is coming, and now is, when the true worshipers will worship the Father in spirit and truth; for the Father is seeking such to worship Him" (John 4:23). He was

clearly welcoming this woman away from her emptiness to be filled with the love of God who seeks the worship of honest hearts like hers.

Item: Paul called the Romans to present themselves as people of worship. Why? "So you can come to know the goodness, the desirability and the perfection of God's purpose in your lives" (Rom. 12:2, author's paraphrase).

The danger of falling prey to anthropocentrism melts when the Word of God is at the center of our thought processes. These brief examples are sufficient to illustrate that, according to God's heart and His Word, worship is for people.

Yet the disposition of Church history works against our pure responses to simple truth. The flow of human traditions seems to go from life to death. So often in institutions the tendency is that the practices giving rise to the life of the organization eventually degenerate until they are being done only for the sake of the doing. Church-based worship is just one casualty of this unfortunate human tendency.

Inertia brings inevitable death. What began with vital life has in too many places become a mere form with only an empty habit remaining.

PEOPLE AS A CENTRAL CONCERN

My worship class worked through their semester reports, accumulating insights and observations which indicated that churches, pastors, buildings, choirs and even liturgies were seldom the cause of ineffective worship. A lost consciousness of people was as much at fault as any lost consciousness of God.

Wherever vital spiritual life was found in a congregation, worship was serving as a means to meet human need. This may have not been the studied perspective in any of those churches, but intentionally or not, people's needs were being met. No one seemed to be using worship as a self-serving tool, and the pristine vision of worship unto the Lord was not being corrupted. Services weren't manipulated to serve human whims, nor was God being expected to jump through a hoop to meet human demands.

I learned a lot with that class. I learned that our fellowship with God in worship was a two-way street: God desires to meet our needs and fulfill us as much as He desires to receive our expressions of praise and thanksgiving.

My perspective on the reason for worship was changed without sacrificing my essential Bible-centeredness or my God-centered approach to worship. But I was clear on this now: With God, *we* are at the center of His concern, even when we worship.

I didn't know how much more there was to learn about it, but I liked the idea of leading people to worship. I liked it more than I ever had before, because I knew I was preparing something in His presence that would mean "fullness of joy" (Ps. 16:11). It wasn't long before I was able to apply these discoveries, establishing the initial emphasis in the small pastorate to which I was soon to be called.

CHAPTER 4

THE KEY TO NEW LIFE

"I wish you'd oil that lock," I said. "I've had a nasty time getting the key
to turn!" The proprietor looked at my key. He smiled, took it and gave me another.
"I should think it will be much easier now that you
have the right one," he said.

Anna and I, along with our four children, accepted the little congregation in Van Nuys about a year later. We were there on temporary assignment while I was still teaching at the Bible college.
Although there were only 18 members and our term of service
was yet uncertain, I was anxious to try what the Holy Spirit had
been making vibrant within me. I was ready to pastor with this

proposition governing my approach to services: *Worship is an opportunity for man to invite God's power and presence to move among those worshiping Him.*

I had also begun to see that since worship is for people, it could also be the key to evangelism. It followed that if God were to "move in"—if He truly wanted to be present in power and bless His people at worship services—then people would be drawn to Christ. The question was, would previously unyielded hearts sense the reality of His presence and open up to Him?

The laboratory of pastoral experience has verified that they do indeed!

We have found that worship is the pathway and the atmosphere for people—the saved and the unsaved alike—to discover

- their royal calling in Christ,
- their high destiny in life,
- their fullest personal worth and
- their deepest human fulfillment.

But here again, tradition must be confronted and questioned and adjustments made if God's maximum benefits are to be realized during worship. I had been ignorant of worship as a means by which God's presence could be welcomed consistently. Consequently, I had grown to depend on preaching alone as the instrument for bringing people to repentance. Suddenly I was discovering a kind of teamwork between the Spirit and the Word—the Holy Spirit softening hearts as we worshiped and the Word opening people's eyes in a new atmosphere of love. This also changed the nature of my appeal to the lost. Invitations, which early in my ministry I had seen as wrestling matches of the will, were now simpler and approached with a different mind-set.

I became convinced that God's program of redemption does not require of any man a ritual denouncing his humanness, though it does require that he renounce his sin. Biblical repentance does not require submission to a predigested, dictated, dehumanizing recitative that blasts the sinner for his sinfulness. However, it does require a full-hearted turning from one's own way to Jesus Christ—to acknowledge ourselves as lost and Him as the only Savior, to acknowledge ourselves as dead in sin and Him as resurrected Lord. The spirit of worship made sure our evangelistic approach was not a humanistic program of self-ascent, while at the same time preempting a theological program of self-debasement.

When worship is warm, it provides the ideal setting for getting evangelistic results. Where "worship is for people," man's highest possibilities are affirmed—truly affirmed as people come before the throne of their Creator.

It is there we *find Him* who created us for joy.

It is there we *find redemption* from all that would destroy or diminish our joy.

Such an approach in worship becomes an honest and humble, yet joyous and hopeful, acknowledgment of

- God's great love for us, verified in His Son, Jesus (see Eph. 2:4,5);
- God's great forgiveness, ensuring acceptance before Him (see Eph. 1:3-6);
- God's great purpose in us, establishing worth and dignity (see Eph. 2:6-10); and
- God's great promises to us, giving confidence for tomorrow (see 2 Pet. 1:4).

Small wonder thousands of souls have opened their lives to Jesus in this worship-filled atmosphere!

AND THEN, GROWTH

As the small pastorate began to grow, the workability of the transformed viewpoint I had gained with my students was becoming inescapably established. Permanent, enduring verification accrued to establish a threefold proposition:

1. Worship is for people.
2. Worship welcomes Kingdom power.
3. Worship is the key to evangelism.

As I led my people in worship—with a commitment to glorify God but with an equal pledge to believe He wanted to save, satisfy and dignify man—true personal fulfillment blossomed in an ever-growing number of people. Moreover, the Holy Spirit began knitting us into a marvelously loving fellowship, for where God's love is responded to, a love for one another overflows. We would sing:

Come, O Lord, and overflow us with Your love,
Come, O Lord, and overflow us with Your love,
For we lift our hearts like vessels
To the everflowing stream.
Come, O Lord, and overflow us with Your love.

And He would do it!

As He did, I was amazed at the remarkable harvest of souls. People were being saved, and the incredible thing to me—having been raised on the notion that evangelistic sermons are essential to evangelistic results—was that *worship* was the source of this mighty moving of the Holy Spirit among us. People were receiving Jesus Christ, not because I preached them under conviction, but because they sensed the presence of God as we worshiped His Majesty. The Word of truth I taught became life in that atmosphere of praise, and that life was begotten in the hearers as the warmth of God's presence invaded our worship.

I am totally persuaded that worship is the key to evangelism as well as to the edification of the Church. Amid childlike, full-hearted worship, God's love distills like refreshing dew upon us. As worship moves beyond a merely objective exercise demanded by theological posturing and as it becomes a simple, subjective quest for God, He responds. He answers the hunger of earnest hearts and reveals Himself in personal, transforming and fulfilling ways. The hungry and thirsty are filled as we seek Him in our worship. In His loving mercy He delights to come into our midst, to ignite His Word, to pour out His Spirit, to breathe His life into those who seek Him and to touch them with His hand of power.

> AS WORSHIP MOVES BEYOND MERE EXERCISE AND BECOMES A SIMPLE, PERSONAL QUEST FOR GOD, HE RESPONDS.

WHO'S INVITED?

Whom do *you* want to come to church, and whom does *God* want there? How you answer this question will determine everything about how you worship God where people gather. If worship is exclusively the privileged right of an approved membership schooled in the acceptable forms of the group, an outsider may be allowed to attend services, but he will essentially remain "outside." The avowed policy that everyone is welcome doesn't stick if the atmosphere of welcome is disallowed—even if it's done unintentionally.

However, when worship is led in such a way as to be accessible to all who come, when an atmosphere of hope and joy is cultivated, then church services become an open doorway, not a guarded fortress.

I submit to you that worship has never been intended by God to be an occasion for proving one's expertise in religion but for satisfying one's hunger and thirst for God.

I believe that Sunday morning was never intended to become a weekly test of personal orthodoxy but was meant to open to all a reservoir of refreshing by way of inspiration, insight and blessing.

I contend that as long as worship is focused on protecting God from unworthy participants, it can never serve His purpose as a resource for incomplete and broken mankind to find completion and wholeness in His presence.

Again, I believe that worship is for people, not the other way around. God does not first *receive* worship; He first *gives* it. Just as the Sabbath was given to allow recreative reprieve for His most noble creation, God has given worship as a means for man's

recovery,

restoration,

reviving,

redemption and
refreshing.

And yet, just as the Pharisees had turned the Sabbath into an impossible system of ritual observance squelching joyous participation by the average person, some in the Church today have elevated the idea and practice of worship to a place few can attain because of the insistent demands of ritual performance or theological expertise.

Sequence is the issue. God's gift is first. God has given worship to everyone as a privileged resource, not as a private regimen to be performed for His scrutiny.

The gathering of people in His name is still intended to be an occasion when hungry and searching souls find an atmosphere of warmth and acceptance.

I've decided to risk the protests of the spiritual purist: "Humanistic! Idolatrous! Anthropocentric! Vanity of vanities!" However, before an explosion of flashing red lights and blaring klaxons disrupts the halls of ecclesiastical orthodoxy, let no one mistake my meaning:

> *In saying worship is* for *man, I have not said that worship is to man. And in saying that worship is a gift to man, I didn't say it isn't to be expressed* unto *God.*

He—the Transcendent and Eternal One—is still the object of our worship and adoration. But in approaching the task of leading worship as I have declared it here, each time I step before my flock, I sense God's pleasure. I am leading them to Him, but I am doing it by means of a *gift* He has given for their blessing. Worship is for *them,* and I learned that they experience growth in every way as they receive this gift of worship as something that is *theirs.*

I think you'll find the same, for thousands who have joined with me in this discovery have come to attest to the vitality of these facts:

1. God has provided worship as a means of entry to our rejoicing in the presence of the Ultimate Reality.
2. Worship introduces dimensions of possibility in every life that transcend our sin and our self-imposed limitations as we welcome the Transcendent One.
3. Worshiping God brings the highest sense of dignity humanity can know, for the regal nature of His Majesty begins to flow downward and inward.

The greatest issue we face as a Church is not so much that we immediately perceive the depth of our sin and weakness or even the greatness of God's grace and power. The primary issue is whether we will come. Will we be led before His throne and seek Him? Because if we do, *heaven will break loose on earth!*

In our church, the passage of three decades has seen tremendous growth—an increase in attendance to nearly 8,000 each week (midweek and Sunday services combined) and a garnering of nearly 65,000 decisions for Christ during that time span—all flowing from this mind-set concerning worship's priority and its purpose.

During those years, time and again in my study of the Scriptures, the Holy Spirit has unveiled to me notable personalities of the Bible whose experiences serve as case studies in the power and purpose of worship. I'd like to share some of these unveilings with you in the following chapters.

CHAPTER 5

FUMBLING FORWARD IN FAITH

The simple beauty in the first tottering steps of a child, overshadowing all absence of grace and form, is seeing the sheer sparkle of joy's adventure in his eyes. The progress is so small but the accomplishment so great.

Abraham is a paradox in terms.

He is honored in the gallery of the faithful in Hebrews 11 despite the fact that he lied about his relationship with his wife, virtually surrendering her body to the whim of a pagan king. He is called the father of faith, but in an effort to beget a promised child, he fathered a problem child—and the diplomacy of world governments is tested to this day as a result (see Gen. 16:11,12). How does it happen that such a human, fallible, fear-filled person gains a reputation for faith?

While watching a televangelist preach on "Boldness and Authority with God" a few years ago, I was somewhat taken aback by his zealous effort on the subject. Of course, I appreciated his intent and I wouldn't presume to criticize his spirit, but I was troubled at his approach.

"I want you to look at Abraham," he exhorted. "Here is a man of faith—the 'father of our faith,' the Bible says. I want you to see the authority of faith that he shows. He gained such a place in God that he entered into consultation with Him as to what God was going to do in great cities. He boldly called on God to rescue Sodom and Gomorrah. Imagine it, saints! One man moving God's hand of action. That's faith. That's boldness. That's authority with God. That's what I'm talking about."

Now, some people might be irritated with every aspect of this preacher's words. The whole idea of such intimacy with and rulership under God is foreign to the perception of many earnest believers. But that isn't what bothered me. I do believe there is a grand arena of possibility for our intercession with God—one that fulfills His higher intentions for us as His sons and daughters. Rather, what disturbed me was the unwitting, but no less actual, dishonesty of the proposition as it was presented. Besides hinting that Abraham's interaction with God was on the order of a brash kid issuing demands to his father, the whole episode was removed from the human context in which the Bible casts this remarkable man. However bold his intercession may have been, the whole story not only depicts Abraham's approach as humbly hesitant, but the next chapter also cites yet another instance of his fumbling humanity.

The same man who is described in Genesis 19 as making a bold appeal for the sparing of cities is seen in the very next chapter trading his integrity and his wife's chastity to save his own neck. This is hardly a picture of an accomplished master of faith!

I strongly resist projections of "the faith life" such as the televangelist made, not because I would discourage a bold, believing lifestyle, but because the Bible doesn't describe such a life as superhuman. There is nothing more self-defeating in the communication of God's call to supernatural living than to suggest a grandiose or contrived, affected piety that is outside the scope of what the Bible actually describes. I like the proposition inherent in the book title *Extraordinary Living for Ordinary Men*, an old book by Sam Shoemaker. God's power in human flesh will hopefully make us less "carnal," but it will never make us less human!

A close examination of Abraham's life does provide great lessons in faith's growth, and the New Testament does hold him forth as faith's "father"—one in whose steps we are to walk (see Rom. 4:11,12). However, this assessment of the patriarch's life is made after the fact—after a lifetime of growth, after the final evaluation of a man's life following his very human earthly sojourn.

Abraham was called; he answered. He learned at times and was blindly doltish at others. He succeeded on some occasions and failed on others—always moving forward in faith but often fumbling as he groped his way through life.

This isn't to demean Abraham or show disrespect for the marvelous witness he left to us. God's Word endorses his life with these words: He "obtained a good testimony through faith" (Heb. 11:39). I'm not suggesting anything less, but I don't believe the testimony of the faithful is given to intimidate us. The stories of men and women of faith are recorded in the Bible in order to build our belief so that *we* can obtain a good testimony through faith!

In Abraham's case, the hallmark of a holy habit merits our study here, for this continuing trait of his helped to bring about his accomplishments in faith. As we look at the whole of Abraham's life, what stands out is this: Whether stumbling, succeeding, fumbling or failing, the one outstanding, discernible feature of his character is that *he lived his life before the altar of God.*

In the dozen pages or so the Bible takes to tell the entire story of Abraham, we see him worshiping at an altar nearly a dozen times. His worshipful walk points the path to understanding how today's believer may also advance in God's will.

It isn't surprising to find in Abraham's life the same issues that God began to remedy in Adam's: a restoration of fellowship and fruitfulness, of relationship and rulership.

In Paul's classic elaboration of justification by faith, Abraham is used as a case study of the gargantuan truth that faith, not works, establishes an individual's relationship with God (see Rom. 4). In this context, the Bible describes Abraham as one who received "the promise that he would be the heir of the world" and that this same promise was also to be "to his seed" (Rom. 4:13). These are prophetic words speaking to us, today's believers. To be a world heir doesn't require the business acumen to control Wall Street or the savvy to succeed in Hollywood; but it does mean we can overcome the ruling spirit of this world and "reign in life" by the power of Jesus Christ's life within us (Rom. 5:17). Thus, Abraham's pilgrimage isn't intended merely as a historical study; it's a model for *our* possibilities, too!

The summary Paul makes of Abraham's life breathes of restored dominion, of recovered rulership. The Word here not only applies those prospects to every believer but also commands us to learn the way to the same by walking "in the steps of the faith [of] our father Abraham" (Rom. 4:12). Upon examination, we find his steps constantly leading to an altar of worship, with each experience teaching us how even the most human and fumbling among us may find his or her inheritance as an "heir of the world."

Abraham's altar experiences unfold like a chain reaction of growth in faith, revealing a worshiping believer who moves forward to possess God's purpose for his life. Though his human fallibility results in periodic fumbling, his call as a world heir is ultimately unimpeded by that humanness as his experiences at God's altar progressively transform him. Abraham is proof that fumbling saints can find their way forward as humanness and holiness converge in the fragility of human flesh.

The Bible shows us several altars in Abraham's experience, his worship-walk offering lessons for our own steps of progress—from first being *called* to a life of faith to our eventual overcoming as victors in faith. Let's look at the principles of how worship moves us forward in faith.

THE FIRST ALTAR: ACCEPTING GOD'S PROMISES

> Then the LORD appeared to Abram and said, "To your descendants I will give this land." And there he built an altar to the LORD, who had appeared to him (Gen. 12:7).

There is an abiding reluctance in every thoughtful person that shies away from promises of personal significance. Only the gullible leap at proposals of impending greatness awaiting them; only the naïve believe without hesitation. Yet I have met hundreds of people who have supposed that because they at first doubt such God-given promises, they were thereby permanently disqualified for faith. But the definition of faith is not wide-eyed gullibility, nor do the promises of God require an instant "go-for-it" reaction.

The first point of faith is simply to be open to God's promise, even when the promise seems beyond our ability to contain it. But there is a better way to respond to God's higher promises than to remain hesitant. We must *take* the promise—receive it, but *take it to the altar of worship*.

Abraham wasn't having delusions of grandeur: *God was speaking to him*. Neither is it a delusion that God still speaks to His people and confirms to their hearts that His Word holds high promise for their own life situations in the here and now. There's no way we can replay the mental processes of Abraham's thoughts to know how closely they parallel our own when grand promise awakens hope in our souls. But we would not be unwise to presume Abraham was shocked by God's word. Although the Bible says, "He did not waver at the promise of God through unbelief, but was strengthened in faith, giving glory to God" (Rom. 4:20), it doesn't say he wasn't surprised. God's call to faith may stun us, but it need not stagger us. Abraham was steadfast but not because he was less vulnerable to doubt than the rest of us; he stood firm because he went to his knees at an altar, "giving glory to God."

This is the first principle of advancing in faith: Worshiping the giver of the promise reminds us of His power to perform and His faithfulness to keep His promises.

THE SECOND ALTAR: LEARNING MORE OF THE PROMISER

And he moved from there to the mountain east of Bethel, and . . . there he built an altar to the LORD and called on the name of the LORD. So Abram journeyed, going on still toward the South (Gen. 12:8,9).

More than a continuing practice of altar-building and worshiping is indicated here. The distinct statement that Abraham called on the name of the Lord points to a growing knowledge of God. The name of the Lord reflects His nature, His person and His character. Abraham was journeying onward, but his travels did more than acquaint him with the tough issues of life; he was also learning the trustworthy nature of his Lord.

Some time ago I was contacted by an irate person who, with temper flaring, attacked the ministry of the church I pastor on the basis of one issue: "A member of your pastoral staff said . . . ," and the person went on to say what the staff member had said and done.

I was appalled.

His wasn't a charge of immorality, financial dishonesty or doctrinal error. The charge was of gross insensitivity toward a person who had called for help. In responding, I didn't retaliate or deny the charge; I simply asked how my present caller knew all that had been said. Although I didn't say it to him, I knew the charge wasn't true. I knew it, not because I

WORSHIP IS THE KEY TO CONQUEST.

was there, not because I presumed perfection among our staff, not because I was defensive, but because I knew the man who was being charged. I knew he was incapable of acting the way that had been described. (Indeed, when the whole matter was resolved, what actually had happened was not even remotely related to the purported facts that had been hurled at me over the telephone.)

There's a parallel reality every one of us faces regularly: the reality that a liar, the Arch-Deceiver, is ever ready to contest the trustworthiness of God, especially when time passes and promises we received from Him have not yet been fulfilled. Trying circumstances sometimes force questions about the strength of our faith—and the certainty of His faithfulness. The Accuser will charge God with faithlessness, bombarding our minds with incriminating remarks, seeking to remove our sense of security in the Father's Word.

When he attacks God's nature or assails our sense of confidence, ongoing and sustained worship is the key to conquest. When I walk each day into His presence, worshiping Him and allowing the Holy Spirit to make Jesus' name—His faithfulness, His healing, His loving, His keeping power—real to me, I will remain steadfast. Knowing more of the Promiser keeps me strong in trusting His promises, even when my hope is attacked and self-doubt seeks to dominate my spirit.

THE THIRD ALTAR: RETURNING TO "GO"

Then Abram went up from Egypt. . . . to the place of the altar which he had made there at first (Gen. 13:1,4).

From the place of his second altar, Abraham seemed to make a detour. His trip to Egypt appeared to be (1) undirected by God,

(2) characterized by compromise and yet (3) climaxed by prosperity, although his new wealth was coupled with expulsion (see Gen. 12:10–13:2).

We could wish for a detailed report filling in the months of Abraham's presumptuous descent into Egypt. The motive is given—there was famine and he sought food—but his method was the pursuit of personal supply in the wisdom of his own way. The resultant compromising of his integrity, involving the exploitation of his wife's beauty, would have brought further failure had not God intervened. However, the interposing sovereign grace drew Abraham back to Bethel and back to worship. Whatever may have been ignorantly lost through his fleshly efforts at self-provision was graciously restored through God's faithful protection—and Abraham worshiped God, having returned to the place of his beginning.

He is not alone in having drifted from God's best through humanly motivated enterprise. However sincere we may have been at certain times, all of us have stepped outside the will of God in well-meaning attempts to solve our own problems. The beauty of studying this event in the life of faith's father is that it holds hope for me. The same God who laid hold of Abraham, though faith faltered and he blindly sought his own way, is the One who today will bring back anyone who will allow it.

In so many games we learned in our childhood, returning to "Start" meant to lose everything one had gained to that point. There are many stumbling believers who feel the same way about God, as though His displeasure with their failures means they are faced with a life of interminable frustration. But where God can find a worshiper whose heart is bent beside his knee at an altar of praise to Him for His mercy and grace, there is a marvelously wonderful promise: "Let the lawless forsake his way and the unrighteous man his schemings. Let him return to the Lord, and He will have mercy on him; and to our God, for He will abundantly pardon" (Isa. 55:7, composite translation of Rheims, Berkeley and *NKJV*).

Abundant pardon! There is no wealth like this reward.

The oft-enjoyed game of Monopoly includes an interesting card that is discovered occasionally when someone lands on "Chance." The card reads: "Return to 'Go'—Collect $200." The irony of the directive is that in one respect it seems to penalize, but in another it rewards. And so it is with God. There may be no way to forget the foolishness of our blind pursuits that end in cul-de-sacs; but the God we began with in worship will seek us there and draw us back to the beginning.

When He does, worship Him at once. He doesn't require a waiting period for returnees—a proving time before their worship is received. He welcomes your worship and your return to fullness just as surely as He did before.

THE FOURTH ALTAR: ENLARGING YOUR HORIZONS

> And the LORD said to Abram, . . . "Lift your eyes now and look; . . . all the land which you see I give to you." . . . Then Abram moved his tent . . . and built an altar there to the LORD (Gen. 13:14,15,18).

The most noteworthy trait of Abraham's worship-walk was that it is always a response. God dealt with him and Abraham worshiped.

In that, there is an unspoken wisdom that might be overlooked unless it is underlined: Worship transcends our weakness while acknowledging God's power.

FUMBLING FORWARD IN FAITH   77

Reestablished in the land, Abraham is later challenged again by the Lord. God had earlier promised this land, but now He begins to specify dimensions—"northward, southward, eastward, and westward. . . . Arise, walk in the land through its length and its width, for I give it to you" (Gen. 13:14,17). What was a general statement that allowed for Abraham's interpretation was now specifically designated, and the boundaries must have been much grander than Abraham had ever imagined.

Abraham's story is one of the believing life.

Whatever joy, blessing and fulfillment any of us has discovered in our early walk with Christ, inevitably we come to a place of confrontation with God. He who will never allow us to stagnate or settle for the small or the shallow, ever draws us to loftier heights and deeper depths.

Have you ever experienced His deeper call to know Him better? Or His higher call to serve Him at new levels? And how have you felt when He calls? Weak? Insufficient? Uncertain? Hesitant?

If so, let us learn together the lesson of Abraham's fourth altar: Worship is the way to receive the promise of possibilities larger than you ever imagined. Worship is the way to respond when you feel you are incapable of all you understand Him to be calling you to. Respond to Him. "Faithful is the One who calls you—He will also accomplish it!" (1 Thess. 5:24, author's paraphrase).

TOWARD WORLD HEIRS

These four scenes from the life of Abraham launch us in applying worship to a walk that moves toward the world-heir life of dominion and restored rulership that Jesus died to give us. To that end, we learn two other power principles from

Abraham's experiences that drew him to the altar of worship:

1. *The principle of worshipful giving in response to the blessings of victory and provision* (see Gen. 14:18-20). Abraham's tithe to Melchizedek acknowledged the Lord as Provider and Possessor of all things, the One from whom he received the privilege of anything he was given and everything he had.

2. *The principle of worship as spiritual warfare* (see Gen. 15:10-21). Abraham's sacrifice was offered to God and attended by a great promise from God concerning the future of Abraham's offspring. The effort of vultures to seize the sacrifice so worshipfully offered and Abraham's rising to drive them away provide a potent picture of the believer's contending in worship against the hosts of hell who seek to overthrow God's purposes for us, our children and our households.

Along with these principles, three events in succeeding chapters of Genesis powerfully demonstrate the developments that might be expected to flow from a maturing worshiper's life. Each event is a worship experience because in each a new submission to God's purpose is learned and a new power in God's kingdom is exercised.

Chapter 17: The exercise of life-begetting power. God calls Abraham to accept the sign of circumcision as a token of the covenant between God and him. He does so at the price of blood, pain and the acceptance of a world which mocked the practice—thereby presenting his body as a living sacrifice unto God (see Rom. 12:1,2) and paving the way for Isaac's birth and the fulfillment of God's promise.

Chapter 18: The exercise of intercessory power. God relates to

Abraham the impending doom of Sodom and Gomorrah, entrusting to this man-of-covenant the possibility of beginning to learn the ruling faith inherent in intercession. Abraham steps out in humility and boldness, and the God he worships unveils His heart of mercy and effects a divine rescue of the few redeemable inhabitants of a reprobated culture.

Chapter 20: The exercise of healing power. God answers Abraham's intercessory prayer for the healing of the women of Abimelech's household—a notable example of Abraham as one who fumbles forward in faith. On the heels of his reverting to earlier fear and compromise, repentance brings a release of great faith and power and opens the door to his ministering a reversal of his sin's consequences.

This progression of a man moving from his first steps in faith to his perception of himself as an intercessor for nations and as a minister of God's healing power is indicative of the fruit of worship. This fruit is not an accidental by-product but a process originating from the divine intent of God. Our focus on worship as the God-given means to return man to rule is simply and practically manifest in Abraham, the father of our faith, whom every New Testament believer is called on to emulate.

WORSHIP'S HIGHEST DOMINION: SURRENDER

But the glory of such a way of victory and dominion cannot be completely learned until we come to Abraham's final lesson in worship. It is here that our greatest understanding of ruling and reigning with Christ occurs—when we come to learn that the highest dominion is gained through our surrender of everything we hold dear.

God tested Abraham, saying:

Take now your son, your only son Isaac, whom you love, and go to the land of Moriah, and offer him there as a burnt offering on one of the mountains of which I shall tell you (Gen. 22:2).

Abraham was called upon to sacrifice his son to his God—an act most of us in this day and age would consider hideous, even barbaric. What God was asking must have seemed a perversion of the Lord's very nature as Abraham understood it. His mind was probably reeling at first as he saddled his donkey for the journey, with reason's thoughts screaming, *Why, God?! Did You not promise this son to me? Will You now take from me my joy?*

But the heart matured through years of worship can quell the mind tormented by one day's turmoil. Abraham knew what kind of God he served and obeyed the Lord, notwithstanding the frightening vision of his only son writhing in death on a pile of wood and surrounded by flames.

Abraham answered the call to worship and, at a place called Moriah, God met him:

Then they came to the place of which God had told him. And Abraham built an altar there
    and placed the wood in order;
    and he bound Isaac his son
    and laid him on the altar, upon the wood.
    And Abraham stretched out his hand and took the
knife to slay his son.
    But the Angel of the LORD called to him from heaven
and said, "Abraham, Abraham!"
    So he said, "Here I am."

And He said, "Do not lay your hand on the lad, or do anything to him; for now I know that you fear God, since you have not withheld your son, your only son, from Me" (Gen. 22:9-12).

It was there that the Lord provided another sacrifice, a ram caught by his horns in a thicket. Abraham gladly offered the ram in place of his son, teaching us that salvation comes by a substitute—a savior dying in our place.

Genesis 22 is a love story and a case study of a world heir entering into his largest inheritance:

- The story reveals God's love for Abraham. He invites him to enter the fellowship of the Father, as one who loves and trusts enough to sacrifice His Son.
- The story reveals Abraham's love for God, refusing to give voice to his doubts even when it appeared that God was about to violate His own nature in requiring human sacrifice.
- The story reveals Isaac's love for Abraham, in his submitted trust that his father would only obey a God who had the best interests of everyone—including Isaac—at heart.

Here is true dominion.

This is worship rising beyond mere power into the fullest dimensions of partnership with God—into "the fellowship of His sufferings, being conformed to His death" (Phil. 3:10). The worshiper may learn to surmount life's obstacles, overcome his own fumbling humanity and move into the exercise of power-with-God, but he must never let the quest for ruling with Christ be separated from worship which acknowledges dying with

Christ. They must be knit together and kept in a balanced perspective, because our ruling with Christ always flows from a partnership of dying with Christ.

And you need not be a religious expert or mystical saint to rise to such a height. A very human "forward-fumbler" can qualify—if he keeps worshiping.

CHAPTER 6

UNSHACKLING YOUR FUTURE

Thine eye diffused a quick'ning ray, I woke, the dungeon flamed with light.
My chains fell off; my heart was free, I rose, went forth and followed Thee.

CHARLES WESLEY

Non sequitur: "What would you rather, or go fishing?"

Non sequitur: "I always thought you had pretty eyes, but isn't the soccer team going to play tomorrow?"

Non sequitur: "Ken called and said the weatherman predicted rain today. I really loved playing marbles when we lived on Lexington Street."

Non sequiturs.

They're those abrupt, illogical turns of thought and speech that have no apparent relationship to one another—remarks that have no bearing on what has just been said. Because non sequiturs are usually indicative of the scatterbrained or the irrational, we don't find them in the Bible. But there is one place where it seems that one occurs. In the middle of a conversation between God and Moses, an exchange takes place that defies logic—unless we are ready to change our thinking about worship.

The setting: Mount Sinai—also called Horeb—the Mountain of God.

The occasion: The commissioning of Moses at the burning bush to go into Egypt and command Pharaoh to release the Hebrew slaves.

Moses asks, "Who am I that I should go to Pharaoh, and that I should bring the children of Israel out of Egypt?" (Exod. 3:11).

The Lord answers, "I will certainly be with you. And this shall be a sign to you that I have sent you: When you have brought the people out of Egypt, you shall serve [worship] God on this mountain" (v. 12).

Read it again. And *listen*.

Question: "Who am I to attempt so great a program of deliverance?"

Answer: "I will be with you: You bring the people here to worship Me."

Non sequitur? It seems like one, doesn't it? Moses' question has to do with his qualifications, but God's answer has to do with the issue of worship. The exchange between the Lord and Moses isn't illogical, but the power in the logic and the lesson it contains cannot be firmly grasped without our confronting a common problem of perspective. We all tend to lack the essential viewpoint, and our usual approach to the book of Exodus demonstrates the need.

THE TROUBLE WITH THE TEN COMMANDMENTS

To the contemporary believer *The Ten Commandments* is not only the decalogue inscribed on tablets of stone but also the title of a motion picture. It is an inescapable problem that probably more people envision the Exodus as portrayed by Cecil B. DeMille than as reported by Moses, the prophet of God. The story's drama serves as the backdrop for an attempt by Hollywood's special-effects artists to recreate the phenomenal and the miraculous—so much grist for the screenwriter's mill. But Exodus always ends in the movieland versions as merely the story of Israel's deliverance from slavery. It's more than that: Exodus is a book about the power and purpose of worship.

I was first struck by the real issue of Exodus when I was jarred by the apparent non sequitur when a bewildered Moses expresses doubt about his own qualifications and God replies, "Bring the people to this mountain." My first reaction was, *God wasn't listening to Moses.* But when I prayed through the text, something clicked and my perspective changed.

Through God's apparently incongruous response I was brought to an awareness that here was hidden the secret of God's purpose for Israel and His key to their destiny. The pathway to His purpose was the pathway to worship. The way of deliverance—of unshackling their future—was not so much an open sea as an awaiting mountain. There they would hear from God and come to know Him as they worshiped Him according to His will and His way.

Let's take a fresh look at Exodus from this viewpoint.

WORSHIP IS THE REAL ISSUE IN EXODUS

"The most dramatic coming-out party in history" may seem an irreverent description of Israel's deliverance under Moses' leadership, but it's certainly an apt one. Just as a young woman of wealthy parentage enters the social scene with a splash of splendor, God shook the status quo of the ancient world and made a statement about His power and His people. He not only drained the resources of the richest monarchy of the time, bringing Egypt to its knees, but also the display of His miraculous power had such an impact that four decades later nations still trembled at the memory of His workings (see Josh. 2:10).

As thrilling and as electrifying as the flow of events is in the first half of Exodus, the sensation turns our attention from the real issue.

Exodus is primarily a study in the power of worship to release people, but it's hard to secure that focus with a Heston-like figure looming above you. Our vision of worship blurs before the onset of overpowering scenes as a towering figure stretches his rod over the storm-tossed sea, miraculously splitting it apart. We envision the same figure coming down the side of Sinai like a giant with a glowing face, gripping stone tablets under one muscular arm, their engraving still steaming from the touch of God's own finger. The overwhelming explosiveness of the plagues and the wonders of God render it somewhat difficult to see worship at the center of Exodus.

But it is.

Worship is the *heart*, the *core*, the *issue*, the *key*, the *destiny*, the *center* and *above all else* in this book. Consider:

Worship is at the heart of Moses' commission: "Bring the people here that they may worship Me." Their release is for the purpose of allowing their worship, and God's promise is to meet them when they do. He is not only calling them forth to liberty, but he is also calling them to intimacy. He is sending a deliverer not only to free them but also to bring them to Himself. Since God enunciates His desire so clearly—to liberate His people that they might come to know His love—it is clear that worship is at the heart of the matter.

Worship is at the core of the message the Lord told Moses to give to Pharaoh:

> And you shall say to him, "The LORD God of the Hebrews has met with us; and now, please, let us go three days' journey into the wilderness, that we may sacrifice to the LORD our God" (Exod. 3:18).

Pharaoh rejected that request not only because he wanted to retain the convenience of slaves but also because he knew that *a people free to worship God can never be bound by earthly powers.* Because the spirit of the world will always seek to retain oppressive power over God's own, worship is at the core of God's message.

Worship is at issue in the power struggle between Pharaoh and God. The monarch's willful resistance to the Almighty's declared purpose rested on his own refusal to honor God: "Who is the LORD, that I should obey His voice? . . . I do not know the LORD, nor will I let Israel go" (Exod. 5:2). But God would have exalted Pharaoh as well as delivered Israel had he listened and obeyed: "For this purpose I have raised you up, that I may show My power in you, and that My name may be declared in all the earth" (Exod. 9:16). Pharaoh had the opportunity to become a worshiper of the Lord God, and had Pharaoh done so he might have become known forever as the greatest emancipator in history.

Instead, he chose to resist God and became a study in hardness of the heart and the losing monarch in one of history's most devastating defeats. In determining whether God's declaration will bring a man blessing or judgment, the question will be resolved by his releasing of a people to worship their God (and whether he will acknowledge God as greater than himself). Worship is at issue.

Worship is the key to Israel's protection from the final plague as well as to the practical provision of nourishment for the first stage of the journey ahead of them. The sacrifice of the Passover lamb renews the ancient blood covenant in force since Adam. Israel's enslavement had doubtlessly reduced the frequency of or removed the practice of sacrifice completely. Many had even given over to the Egyptian systems of worship; blood on their doorways certainly subjects them to mockery. But it also declares their faith and ensures their deliverance. Worship is the key.

Worship is the destiny of this people. Following their arrival at Sinai, the Lord says:

> You have seen what I did to the Egyptians, and how I bore you on eagles' wings and brought you to Myself. Now therefore, if you will indeed obey My voice and keep My covenant, then you shall be a special treasure to Me above all people; for all the earth is Mine. And you shall be to Me a kingdom of priests and a holy nation (Exod. 19:4-6).

God's objective in liberating the Hebrew slaves, vanquishing the Egyptians and bringing His people to Sinai is to establish a special relationship: "I brought you to Myself. You shall be a special treasure to Me." Within this covenant relationship will unfold a national destiny—a priestly ministry to the world. Here is to rise a "kingdom of priests"—the one people on the earth who will not only worship God for themselves but who will also serve as priests to lead others to do the same. Worship is their destiny.

Worship is at the center of their lives. The many months at Sinai are given to the structuring of a magnificent mobile worship center: the Tabernacle. It is not a great hall for the assembling of multitudes but a place of personal encounter where worshipers may bring their covenant offerings. "And let them make Me a sanctuary [a sacred place], that I may dwell among them. And there I will meet with you, and I will speak with you" (Exod. 25:8,22). The arrangement of their tribes located three clans each to the north, east, south and west, with the Tabernacle in the middle of them all. God Himself directed their tribal arrangement so that worship was at the center.

Worship is over and above all in the calendar the Lord outlined for the newly enfranchised society of former slaves. Their calendar was built upon weekly sabbaths of worship, monthly new moons of worship and seasonal feasts of celebrative worship. With this, the year is twice highlighted by special "beginnings": the Passover to commemorate their deliverance and the Day of Atonement to sustain the focus of their attention toward holiness of heart and life. Further, the invitation of their offerings of gold, silver, jewels and other precious objects for the building of the Tabernacle, along with their offerings of meal, oil and animals, all form an essential part of their redeeming fellowship with God. There is no part of their life unaffected by worship, and when the Tabernacle was set in place, God crowned it all. The glory of the Lord filled the Tabernacle, and as they would travel the cloud of God rose above, both for their direction and their protection. Worship was over and above all.

REFORMING OUR PERSPECTIVE

My personal confrontation with the real issue in Exodus led to the above conclusions. What I had previously viewed as a non sequitur was the result of my orientation to think of serving God as something I *did* rather than something I was to *be*—that *working* was service rather than *worshiping*. A fresh analysis of Exodus had outlined the relationship between deliverance and worship—the second being the key to the first. Once I came to understand that, God's purpose for His redeemed people came clearer: "And you shall be to Me a kingdom of priests and a holy nation" (Exod. 19:6).

God had intended Israel to become a kingdom of priests. His original plan was that they become a nation of worship leaders, all of them helping and teaching the peoples of the world to understand His heart and ways and to worship Him. The substance and style of their worship was intended to show all mankind the way to God, and therefore worship was the intended vehicle for fulfilling their mission of evangelizing—that is, bringing people into the light of God's love. This was never realized.

The incident of the golden calf dissolved this plan. The breakdown occurred at the foot of the same mountain where God had called His people to learn of their purpose. The goal had been for a *whole nation* to serve as a priesthood *to the nations*. Now, with sin seeping in at the edges, Moses calls out for repentance: "Who is on the Lord's side?" (see Exod. 32:26). The plan could have been reinstated, but sadly and significantly, only one tribe answers the call. As a result of Levi's response, the Levites *alone* became the priestly tribe. The sad result is that an entire nation intended for global priesthood is reduced to a sinning people, barely able to sustain their own spiritual life. A self-serving cycle is set in motion. They end up merely managing their own worship instead of leading the world to the worship of its Creator.

Worship was the means of their deliverance.

Worship was to be their realized destiny—the key to throwing off their chains and unshackling their future.

But the glory that might have been, never was. It would have to wait for people of another era who would learn from the mistakes of their ancestors and finally unleash the highest purposes of God.

THE NEW PRIESTHOOD

The New Testament seems to churn with statements about a people whose unfulfilled destiny had not yet been realized. Jesus describes God's continued search for a people who will worship Him "in spirit and truth" (John 4:24). Time and again, Paul declares that a new era awaits the Church—an unfolding secret of divine destiny, confounding hell and populating heaven.

The promises set forth in the New Testament indicate a people whose worship invites the kingdom of God in a present visitation of power and whose ministry is to

WORSHIP IS OUR MEANS OF DELIVERANCE— THE KEY TO THROWING OFF OUR CHAINS AND UNSHACKLING OUR FUTURE.

declare the kingdom of God as an eternal hope. Two verses seem to embrace the prospect of destiny fulfilled at long last:

> Now all these things happened to them as examples, and they were written for our admonition, upon whom the ends of the ages have come (1 Cor. 10:11).

> And all these, having obtained a good testimony through faith, did not receive the promise, God having provided something better for us, that they should not be made perfect apart from us (Heb. 11:39,40).

The first directs us to learn from Israel's wilderness errors; the second reminds us that the new covenant holds forth possibilities in the Holy Spirit that were not present under the old. The first text shouts, "Don't fall prey to the lust and confusion that ruins the priestly role of the whole people"; the second says, "Welcome the Holy Spirit's indwelling and overflowing to energize your life and expand your worship."

With these directives in mind, today's Church could begin something reformational. We could begin to revive the destiny God intended for His delivered people long ago. His call and mission for a kingdom of priests is still meant to be realized. Its fulfillment simply hinges upon our will to let a reformation in worship transform our thinking and lifestyle.

THE WEAKNESS OF WORSHIP

This reformation began for me when I started to look at worship differently. I was forced to acknowledge that I had not seen worship:

- at the heart of our commission, as it was Moses';
- at the core of our approach to the world's power system;
- at issue in our struggle with principalities and powers;
- as the key to our personal deliverance and destiny;
- as the goal of our being and becoming;
- as the central focus of our church's life; or
- as being over and above all in practical, sacrificial ways.

I was willing to allow worship a place.

I was willing to acknowledge its need and even its desirability.

But at the bottom line I found I had to struggle with my convictions about the relative power of worship in terms of changing, reaching, confronting or *saving* the world. I now confess I had a great deal more confidence in evangelism strategies and logic in preaching than I did in the miracle of worship. Thus, I viewed worship more as a *part* rather than as the *point* of the Church's being. Worship was the gentle lady we escorted on Sunday morning, but our systems were the business heavyweights we depended on to get the job done.

Let's face it. Historically, seldom has worship been considered to be the Church's strength, let alone its front line of power. Worship will never make points in the world system. The world operates on the brawn of bucks, bodies and bombs. But God operates on the power of praise, sacrifice and humility of heart. He works with

submitted souls,

singing saints and

Spirit-filled sanctuaries.

During the intervening years since my own confrontation with the need to prioritize worship, I have discussed this belief with many people. I'm now of the opinion that any reticence toward a reformation in worship isn't merely because of a lack of perspective. I wonder how many of us simply fear the possibility that if we allowed our worship to be transformed, God's power might actually manifest itself in a way we would be unable to control.

But we must let go.

Where once the Lord sent His deliverer to Pharaoh with the message "Let My people go," I believe today he would say to His Church, "My people, let go!"

Any Pharaoh in our own souls must be slain, for Israel's exodus speaks to today's Church, saying that worship is the key to unshackling our future. People who are led to worship God will be delivered to realize their destiny. The path that Israel walked before awaits those who will test its full potential: *Let God's people put worship at the center of their lives, and the glory of God will fill the house where they gather*. When it does, others will behold God in their midst and will be drawn to Him.

We must break free of the notion that today's "Exodus people," the Church, can become truly powerful by strength of arm or human wisdom. Moses' murder of the Egyptian hastened nothing of God's deliverance. And while golden calves heed the world's tastes in worship styles, a people of priestly kingdom power will never be established that way.

Make no mistake, these lessons point to worship as our strength. I must reject the idea that either my strength (Moses' undue zeal) or my style (calves based on Egyptian models) is the key to influence and accomplishment. Worship is what unlocks the doors to the highest release of Christ's purpose among His people. Worship welcomes God's presence; and therein the glory of the Lord is revealed, and "all flesh [everyday human beings] shall see it together" (Isa. 40:5).

WHEN FLESH BEHOLDS GLORY

"I walked in and the instant I stepped through the door I knew I had come home."

"I was sitting there surrounded by the singing, and when you gave the invitation I discovered I was raising my hand in response."

"I listened as the worship time continued—I knew none of the songs but I couldn't stop crying. Peace filled my soul because I knew God was in this place."

"My wife and I had come as a last-ditch effort at keeping our marriage together. We couldn't explain why, but the presence of the Lord was so strong we were changed in our attitude toward Him and toward each other."

Remarks like these fill letters to my office and comments from our congregation. They are case studies in people seeing their futures unshackled. They simply arrived to find a worshiping church—an approach to ministry I had once thought too weak to be workable. But even though the weakness of form and style seemed deficient as a means of impressing either visitors or members, the power of God infused the place to which they had come. Human wisdom, skill or accomplishment was not the pivotal means of securing results that unshackled people and released a whole church to become what God intended.

Could this be what God meant when He said to Moses, "I will have a people who is a nation of priests to the world"? Could these responses be the end result of what God meant when He said, "Bring the people to worship me and I will lead them to a land of fulfillment and a life of purpose"?

I think so.

And even though I had thought God's answer to Moses' question was a non sequitur, I discovered that His answer,

"Bring the people to worship Me," was the right answer, even if it defied human logic.

Worship usually does.

CHAPTER 7

ROYAL BRIDGE BUILDING

The eleventh commandment is, "Thou shalt not sweat it!"

ROY HICKS

There is something about the word "priest" that seems to unsettle most people.

If they're materialists, "priest" seems entirely irrelevant.

If they're Protestants, "priest" seems categorically Catholic.

If they're laymen, "priest" seems "beyond me."

To Joe Anybody, the man on the street, the word "priest" may evoke a spread of feelings from suspicion to reverence—

from prejudice to respect. For others "priest" may awaken memories or experiences that renew the highest esteem or the deepest frustration.

The idea of a priest, in many minds, leans toward the impractical and the mystical, conjuring up notions of otherworldliness or virtual passivity toward everyday realities.

All that, in spite of *pontifex*.

Pontifex is the Latin word for priest. The beauty of the word is that by its actual derivation it makes clear that priest is an active idea, its history revealed in a word of positive and powerful purpose. The real meaning lies in the original definition of "pontifex": "bridge builder." The etymology of the word undergirds such English words as "pons" (a bridge), "pontage" (the toll for crossing the bridge) and "pontoon" (a floating bridge). I dwell on all this to establish a point: Priesthood was always meant to be something practical—to help us cross over, or to get from here to there.

That's one of the reasons "priesthood" was one of the fighting words of the Reformation. The Reformers recognized that the priesthood had become a barricade to God rather than a bridge—a blockage instead of a blessing. The Church's oppressive control over the laity had bred horrible confusion and bondage. The confessional was corrupted through manipulation of the multitude, and sin was licensed through the sale of indulgences. The trumpet call to rally every believer to the awareness of his own priestly role before God was based on the great Reformation text, "The just shall live by faith" (Rom. 1:17). That awakening recovered the truth of the priesthood of the believer. The privilege of access to God at a personal level was affirmed in Christ as people rediscovered their right to come to God with no need for a human mediator of divine blessing (see 1 Tim. 2:5). The bridge-building idea in "priest" was registered again. Priesthood was once again viewed as a personal, practical privilege.

With praise to God for what that era recovered, I believe we are ripe for a new reformation concerning the believer's priestly ministry. I see an awakening about to extend the practical potential of our priestly function as believers. Five hundred years ago the issue was *relationship*—restoring personal access *to* God. Today it is *worship*—revealing the potential in our praises *before* God.

PRIESTS WHO REIGN

The Word of God directly links the two offices of king and priest, merging them into one and calling every believer to function in that joint role:

> To Him who loved us and washed us from our sins in His own blood, and has made us kings and priests to His God and Father, to Him be glory and dominion forever and ever. Amen (Rev. 1:5,6).

The importance of our being awakened to this dual calling—priestly kings and kingly priests—is that it places worship at the heart of God's program for restoring man's dominion. Our role as worshiping priests is the means to our role as reigning kings: "But you are a chosen generation, a royal priesthood, a holy nation, His own special people, that you may proclaim the praises of Him who called you out of darkness into His marvelous light" (1 Pet. 2:9).

The words "kingdom" and "royal" in this text clearly indicate a regal aspect to the priestly ministry of worship. Thus, at the core of our life in Christ is a summons to recognize that our dominion *in* Him directly relates to our worship *of* Him. God's original plan that Israel become "a kingdom of priests" (Exod. 19:6)—a plan that was short-circuited when His people rejected it at Sinai—is now able to be fulfilled in the Church. The priestly mission to lead the nations of the world to God by becoming a people of worship has been reissued.

The power of worship to accomplish God's will is only beginning to be freshly understood. Today's new reformation comprises a people just beginning to learn that Kingdom dominion—the rule of God's almightiness—is introduced into life situations and settings as God responds to the worship of His people:

> For the eyes of the LORD run to and fro throughout the whole earth, to show Himself strong on behalf of those whose heart is loyal to Him (2 Chron. 16:9).

God's response to our worship is not a case of His demonstrating His power just because we make Him feel good. Worship is not the stroking of a juvenile divine ego, nor is it the practice of a priestly magic eliciting marvelous, cosmic powers. What the priest-king role of worship does do is build a bridge between heaven's throne and earth's need. Worship welcomes God's rule into man's circumstances. Because we the redeemed are privileged to be the ones exercising the action which issues that welcome, a regal role is ascribed to us by God Himself. It is again as it was in the beginning: Man's assignment to rule may be regained because his responsibility to worship has been reclaimed.

The early believers were first to discover the priority of worship as the key to recovering world dominion under God's will. They were at worship when the first great breakthrough in global evangelism took place:

> Now in the church that was at Antioch there were cer-
> tain prophets and teachers. . . . As they ministered to the
> Lord and fasted, the Holy Spirit said, "Now separate to
> Me Barnabas and Saul for the work to which I have
> called them." Then, having fasted and prayed, and laid
> hands on them, they sent them away (Acts 13:1-3).

This thrusting forth of those two men from Antioch is as striking an event as any in the Scriptures. It shaped the world forever and set the direction of history's flow. And it occasioned the turning of a corner into an era of Kingdom expansion that continues to this day. However, what usually goes unnoticed is the fact that this small group's strategy for global missionary enterprise was not the product of human ingenuity. It was born simply as humble believers sought God in worship, fulfilling a priest's ministry described since Aaron's time as "ministering to the Lord" (see Ezek. 44:15, for example).[1]

Now may be the hour when the Church most needs this reforming truth.

With the technological, media and mechanical resources available, there is a greater temptation than ever for spiritual leaders and congregations to attempt to accomplish the work of God by the resources of man. We have always had a frightening tendency to mechanize spiritual enterprise in our zeal to achieve more for God's kingdom. However, something else is being accentuated by the Holy Spirit today. He is directing our appointment to priestly worship for the release of Kingdom advancement. A new contingent of priests is being enlisted—
every believer is being called anew to dynamic worship.

Answering that call ought not be feared; this is not a forced retirement from sensible, practical, businesslike behavior. The priestly mission to worship is not to resign responsible duty but to acknowledge that whatever we seek to *do* for God cannot exceed what we are to *be* before Him.

What He has called us to be first is priests—praisers!

In Him also we have obtained an inheritance, being predestined according to the purpose of Him who works all things according to the counsel of His will, that we first trusted in Christ should be to the praise of His glory (Eph. 1:11,12).

You also, as living stones, are being built up a spiritual house, a holy priesthood, to offer up spiritual sacrifices acceptable to God through Jesus Christ (1 Pet. 2:5).

It is difficult, without seeming rather mystical, to elaborate on how the bridge-building ministry of priestly worship and praise is the most practical thing today's Church can learn. Someone reading this book is sure to think I am calling for misty-eyed worship to replace clear-headed thinking.

That can happen, of course, but it isn't God's way and it certainly isn't my point.

Through worship we access the finest of everything, for when we worship, a route between the invisible and the visible is established. When God invades the scene of our praise and visits us with His grace and power, His working does not overlook the obvious:

- Worship is not a substitute for the teaching and preaching of the Word. It does precede it, however, and sometimes is entwined with it. Worship expands the possibilities of preaching because it establishes an atmosphere of respondency to God's will. The revelation of the inspired Holy Scriptures is ignited to life: illuminated and unveiled, the truth *lives* among us!

· The kind of worship I'm talking about is not an attempt to escape from attention to administrative practicality or mundane responsibility. Still, when we learn to frame our business day in worship, discovering the importance of preceding all we do with praise (as opposed to a quick "bless us" prayer), we will find that a remarkable improvement in efficiency can be realized!

I think a broader awareness of the believer's priesthood *in worship* is a fulfillment of certain Old Testament prophecies given by Ezekiel and Jeremiah.

DON'T SWEAT IT

"Thou shalt not sweat it!"

I chuckled at the punchline given by the voice on the phone. The setup question had been posed by a fellow pastor: "Have you heard the Eleventh Commandment?"

Roy Hicks and I had been talking about our joyous experiences since both our congregations were growing so miraculously—his in Eugene, Oregon, and mine in Southern California. What humbled us both was how it had all occurred so rapidly and so easily, without promotion or fanfare on our parts. We were very conscious of the fact that a renewal in worship was at the heart of this growth. That was the context of his "Eleventh Commandment" crack.

It was a direct reference to our mutual concern that we not get in God's way. Our background and experience inclined us both toward energetic promotionalism. But having begun to find a better way—God's way!—we felt cautious that neither of us become even inadvertently guilty of substituting "sweat" for the priestly service of praise to God.

Roy's remark was derived from an explicit directive that God gave Ezekiel. It concerned the clothing to be worn by those priests who would serve God's Temple at a future day: "They shall not clothe themselves with anything that causes sweat" (Ezek. 44:18).

Commentators differ widely on the meaning and timing of Ezekiel's predictions of a final Temple to be built unto God in the last times.[2] However, none preempts a present fulfillment of the prophet's vision in its immediate, spiritual sense. The stream of blessing that Ezekiel saw bursting from under the Temple threshold is clearly a forecast of a great river of refreshing at the last times. Some students believe it is one of the texts Jesus was alluding to as He spoke of the breaking forth in "rivers of living water" when He would come and fill every believer with the Holy Spirit (see Ezek. 47:1-6; John 7:37-39).

Jeremiah elaborates the same concept of a worldwide dimension of blessing—a flowing together of people in praise at a great future time of visitation:

> Therefore they shall come and sing in the height of Zion, streaming to the goodness of the LORD . . . their souls shall be like a well-watered garden, and they shall sorrow no more at all (Jer. 31:12).

In New Testament terms, the reference to Zion does not require a pilgrimage to Jerusalem. The words of Ezekiel and Jeremiah clearly and biblically relate to today, as verified by the way the writer of Hebrews places *every* believer in Zion *every time* we worship: "For you have not come to [Sinai]. . . . But you have come to Mount Zion and to the city of the living God, the heavenly Jerusalem . . . to Jesus the Mediator of the new covenant" (Heb. 12:18-24).

This prophesied priestly awakening which we are seeing today is something of a very real reformation and is occasioning a breakthrough in ministry and in spiritual lives. The Holy Spirit of God is showing us the way to move all ministry beyond mere activities—those sweat-generating pursuits of fruitless tradition and soul-wearying churchmanship.

MUCH WORK, MUCH WORSHIP

I was so stirred on this theme that the Holy Spirit gave me a powerful analogy with which to exhort our congregation:

God has given us *much work* to do as a people. Therefore, our foremost task is to become a people of *much worship*. Worship must *precede* all, and all must *proceed* with worship. Biblical terminology calls a congregation a "body," and as a body we would be wise to pursue our mission in the light of a practical point related to "bodies": Bodies perspire. It has nothing to do with sin; it's just our physical nature. But I think that suggests a lesson about worship.

Church bodies tend to labor with perspiration-producing earnestness. That's no sin either. But before *all* our bodies, worship is the fragrance with which we must cover ourselves. Just as a human body appropriately prepares itself with colognes, deodorants and perfumes, lest the unpleasantness of the natural odor produced by

WORSHIP IS GARNERING A HARVEST!

working causes the body to become objectionable, so the Body of the Church must precede its God-appointed tasks with the supernaturally sweet savor and incense of worship. It's our only security against the smell of the flesh tainting the atmosphere wherein God seeks to display His glory.

Worship is basic to the most rapid advancement of the kingdom of God. It is central because Kingdom power is never generated by the energy of the flesh, but rather it is *released* by the power of the Holy Spirit. The priestly ministry of the believer is crucial and necessary because our dominion as kings rises from our worship as priests, and because it makes room for God's miracle power without leaving a place for flesh to rush to seek the glory. It welcomes the Holy Spirit's distribution of gifts while avoiding Corinthian carnality or confusion.

As we grow in our grasp of God's Word, we are fueling the fires of a reformation in worship—a recognition that what began nearly five centuries ago has not exhausted the richness of the meaning inherent in the words "the priesthood of the believer." With the new awakening to priestly ministry, Christians everywhere are opening up to allow for a biblical release in worship. As they do, it seems a new era of evangelism is beginning to take place. Worship is garnering a harvest!

- Leighton Ford described his amazement at a discovery he made in India, where unbelievers were opening their homes at the request of Christians "that we might use your house for a worship service." With that request, homes opened out of interest and curiosity, with the results that many have received the gospel. But the amazing thing was that their readiness to do so was on the basis of their merely seeing Christians worshiping the Lord.

- Mrs. David Watson, wife of the late beloved rector in York, England, has employed an unusual worship tactic. She has often led groups of the congregation's children through the park near their church, *dancing* their praise to God! As a result, many outsiders have been immediately attracted to the church service—even as the children danced in childlike abandon. Once there, the visitors experienced the congregation at worship and were led to salvation.

- Youth With A Mission has taken worship teams into the streets of Amsterdam, where the jaded tastes of the worldly wise, carnally sated and intellectually defiant have proven resistant to the claims of the gospel. Yet as worshipers simply lifted their voices in song, hearts have melted before God as the Holy Spirit invaded the marketplace where worship had prepared a place for His workings.

• In our own congregation, there have been frequent occasions when I have followed an extended period of worship and praise with a simple invitation to receive Christ. It is not uncommon to experience a dozen or more people at a time opening up to the love of God and becoming established in Christ—drawn by the Holy Spirit working through the spirit of worship.

The remarkable thing about these examples is that they do not involve especially skilled performances. Of course, the musicians practiced and the dancing children rehearsed; but these occasions did not feature the unusually gifted as, for example, at a gospel music concert. As valid as the latter may be in evangelism, that is not what I am describing here. I am talking about the sheer power of praise and worship to introduce the rule of God's kingdom power—that thereby hearts are touched at deep dimensions, and salvation and deliverance are made manifest.

PRIESTS AND KINGS AT HOME

Believers are beginning to learn the power of worship when applied to the everyday routine of their personal lives and circumstances. This is not only contributing to the rise of homes filled with a holy happiness, but it is also resulting in homes where the presence of God's kingdom crowds out the efforts of hell to erode peace and the unity of families.

Chuck was attending one of the Men's Growth Seminars we conduct each month for the gentlemen of our congregation. I had taught on the power of praise as a man's means for exercising his priestly role as spiritual leader of his home. I based my talks on God's instructions to Abraham to walk through the length and breadth of the land promised him (see Gen. 13:17). I proposed that as Abraham's spiritual sons, we should do the same thing.

"How about walking the boundaries of your property, however large or small it may be?" I suggested. "As the priest and leader of your family, sing the praise of the Lord as you do it. Welcome the rule of His kingdom to reign over all and throughout your household."

Chuck went home and shared the teaching with his wife, Judy, and they decided to take the simple truth in the literal way I had proposed: to apply it with worshiping faith to their situation. They had been having a very real problem with one of their teenage daughters and had reached the end of their own ability to deal with the situation. The next day Chuck rose before daylight, not wanting his walking the boundaries of their lot to be seen and thought foolish or superstitious by their neighbors. With songful praise and worship, he circled the perimeter of his lot, believing that God's timeless ways apply today.

"Later that day," Judy said, "while I was working in the kitchen, I felt the strongest prompting to go to Katy's room. As I walked down the hall, praying for her, I felt directed to open the top right-hand drawer of her dresser and reach to the back, beneath the things in the drawer. I did so and without probing at all—simply doing as I felt directed—my hand came upon a cellophane bag. When I removed it, I was shocked. It contained marijuana."

Without detailing the story further, the thrilling outcome centered on Katy's response that evening after school when

Chuck and Judy confronted her. She began weeping and express-ing her gratitude to God for leading her mom to the package.

"Mom . . . Dad . . . You can't know how happy I am this hap-pened! You know I've never done anything like this, and I didn't want to now. I know I've been giving you trouble but not this bad.

"One of the kids at school gave me that bag to get me to con-sider trying it. Even though I didn't, I did keep it. I knew it was all wrong; but in my rebellion I thought that if I kept it available, I might decide later to risk it."

Between sobs she welcomed her parents' prayers with her as she confessed this and other sins. On the spot she returned to an obedient walk with Christ. For Chuck and Judy's part, it is sim-ply a demonstration of the power of worship and praise when introduced into the home.

Is this kind of thing superstition? Coincidence? Fanaticism?

Not at all! Not when the spiritual intent of the old covenant's priestly ministry has been transferred to New Testament believers as we've studied.

If Aaron's bearing the family names of the tribes upon his shoulders before the Lord every day held intercessory signifi-cance with God then (see Exod. 28:12), the glory of the New Covenant holds at least as much for those who come with wor-ship and name their family daily before the heavenly throne.

If Aaron's rushing with incense into the midst of the plague of judgment actually stopped its spread (see Num. 16:46-50), it's not unlikely or presumptuous to expect today that the incense of God's people at prayer and worship could effect a reversal of the destruction ripping cities and nations apart.

Today, the reformation truth of the priesthood of the believ-er is being broadened and heightened. It is expanding worship as the concept is understood—built on the solid ground of God's Word. More and more are coming to relish and respond to the wealth of meaning in their priestly function, as praise and worship are being applied with priestly effectiveness today.

Worship has the power to penetrate hearts, for the childlike beauty and authenticity of true worship bypasses resistant minds and touches souls with the tender reality of God's presence.

Worship has the ability to neutralize the power of demonic attack upon the people of God, for wherever the spirit of praise resides, God is enthroned and neither flesh nor devil can successfully perpetuate its designs.

The new reformation in worship is advancing. The royal priesthood of the believer in Christ is beginning to accomplish what it was ordained to do: extend God's rule through worship.

This is bridge building—spanning the limits of man's circumstance and with worship welcoming the entry of God's unlimited rulership. It's a new government bringing the Spirit of life into a decaying world. This reformation is causing a revolution which, similar to another one before it, is seeking "to secure the blessings of liberty for ourselves and for our posterity." Those words were written by men willing to experience a revolution in order to extend that blessing.

The new reformation in worship invites us to do the same.

CHAPTER 8

SAM'S SONG OF RENEWAL'S WAYS

Let all the past be but a holy prelude, Lord, To the mighty fire and power
You now outpour on me. All-consuming flame come and overflow me,
And let Thy Kingdom come unto me this hour.

The most unsung hero of the Old Testament is Samuel.

He bridged two eras—from the judges to the kings.

He lived in purity while a declining priest bred a decadent household.

He immortalized obedience in the midst of a relativistic society.

He ordained the king destined to sire the Messiah and foreshadow His rule.

Samuel is a study in simple obedience without fanfare, of commitment without apparent reward, of faithfulness to duty when no one else much understood or cared.

Samuel is a study in the ways of transition—the ways of renewal.

SAM'S SONG

Hannah was tortured by barrenness, the affliction of childlessness that caused any ancient Hebrew woman to doubt her worth and wonder about her favor with God. Though well loved by her husband, Elkanah, she longed for a child. This brought her near despair, and as so often is the case when human beings turn to God in their plight, that despair begat a song of hope. It began with prayer and became music.

Her prayer for a child was answered, and upon Hannah's next visit to the Tabernacle, now situated in Shiloh since Israel had entered the land nearly 300 years before, she worshiped the Lord and said:

> My heart rejoices in the LORD;
> My horn is exalted in the LORD.
> I smile at my enemies,
> Because I rejoice in Your salvation.
> No one is holy like the LORD,
> For there is none besides You,
> Nor is there any rock like our God (1 Sam. 2:1,2).

Her song continues for a full 10 verses in the second chapter of 1 Samuel, preserved there by her son's pen as a commemoration of his own birth. One might call it "Sam's Song," the melody of a woman whose God had reversed her situation.

Revolution.

Samuel is an example of God at work overturning the verdicts of a lower court. Just as surely as Samuel was an instrument of Israel's turning from an era of political and moral lawlessness during the time of the judges, and returning from the spiritual emptiness during Eli's high priestly rule, "Sam's Song" connotes God's ways to cause a revolution.

Renewal. Resurrection. Restoration.

These are key words in God's methods for reordering things. Human revolutions may change existing orders and power structures, but they usually carry the excess baggage of bitterness, resentment, retaliation and bloodletting. Instead, when we tune in to Hannah's song as she revels in her restoration from barrenness, we are reminded that "by strength no man shall prevail"; that the Lord is the One who "lifts the beggar from the ash heap to set [him] among princes and make [him] inherit the throne of glory" (1 Sam. 2:8,9).

The components of Hannah's situation, Samuel's birth and Israel's movement toward the king whom God had in mind may be significantly analogous to ours. Just as she longed for a birth, I have met so many who truly long for spiritual renewal. And as her child led the way to the anointing of God's chosen king, David, so those seeking renewal are on track to realizing a new entrance to God's kingdom with love and power. A closer examination of this parallel holds worthwhile lessons, and to begin, Samuel's life and leadership style reveal at least three points to teach any of us who seek God's ways into renewal.

THE DIFFICULTY IN RENEWAL

A person's *passion* for renewal and its practical *possibility* are often miles apart and radically different. It's one thing to hunger for a reformation and quite another to have one. Not everyone enjoys the possibilities that I did when I came to an almost nonexistent congregation of 18 members whose average age was over 60.

Although I was a young pastor, I was also well thought of in my denomination, and this disposed the handful of members I inherited to give me the benefit of the doubt. Thus it was that I experienced virtual hands-off freedom in leading them forward. No substantial built-in structures obstructed the path. I was hopeful of discovering the possibilities in ministry of worship, and they were so few in number that they were glad to have a pastor at all. Moreover, they were not a resistant people anyway, so resistance was out of the question.

That is rarely the case.

I constantly meet pastors and laymen who recognize that a worship reformation is in progress and they want to be a part of it. They are motivated by more than novelty or a quest for success. They genuinely want to be center-stream in the flow of the Holy Spirit to today's Church.

But . . . they face resistance.

Sometimes it's found only in pockets of the congregation they love. At other times it's orchestrated from the grass roots throughout every level of leadership in the local church. Sometimes it's possible to discuss the subject of the congregation's need for renewal; other times such discussion is deemed the equivalent of challenging the truth of the virgin birth. What can be done when you're in such a dilemma?

First, we can always find support in the Lord, just as Hannah did.

God has a heart for people who hunger for renewal.

His faithfulness will always pour forth the fulfilling answer to those who "hunger and thirst for righteousness" (Matt. 5:6). Still, it is important to remember that whenever readiness on our part is not matched by a readiness among others, He is their God, too. His patience with those who fear renewal—even those who resist it—will often require His waiting longer than you or I want to wait. So many of us want to get on with it *right now!* But we would do well to consider the difference between God's *renewing* ways and man's *revolutionary* methods. Samuel's life is a good study in the spirit of faithfulness exhibited by someone who longed to see God's rule instituted but who had to wait to see it accomplished in God's way and in His timing.

BE CHILDLIKE, NOT CHIDING

The story of Samuel's boyhood breathes a quality of childlikeness worthy of our emulation. At a very early age Samuel was brought and dedicated by Hannah and Elkanah to the service of the Tabernacle. Under Eli's training and care, Samuel was subject to the high priest for several years of his early life—years marked by little other than his mother's annual gift to him of a new robe. It was a miniature *ephod*—a priestly order of garb designed for his ministry before the Lord.

During these same years, Eli's own sons were living corruptly, despoiling pure worship at the Tabernacle, seducing women who came there, serving their own greed and gluttony by stealing from the sacrifices brought by the people. Worst of all, these disrespectful young men rejected their aged father's repeated efforts at correcting them.

Eli, weakened from severe obesity, weariness of years and despair over his rebellious sons, seems to epitomize any situation needing renewal. Meanwhile, young Samuel is clearly picturesque of the new—the freshly available, God-ordained rule of the Holy Spirit that makes renewal possible.

If ever a situation cried out for revolution, this travesty in the Tabernacle was one. But God's wisdom and patience, modeled in Samuel, may teach us if we will listen: The way to renewal is to be childlike, not chiding. He points the way to cultivating a reformation without grumping about its need or thumping our Bibles and pulpits and pronouncing our discerning perspective on the situation.

There is a distinct grace in being able to continue in the middle of a situation that needs revival, deliverance or salvation—and remaining both tender in heart and constant in growth. Something about Hannah's year-to-year gift of a new robe for Samuel, joined to the phrase "but Samuel ministered before the LORD, even as a child" (1 Sam. 2:18), presents us with a lesson in patience. God does not require our assistance to force Him into situations that seem to have crowded Him out. He only needs someone who will continue to keep freshly robed for worship—those who with simplicity of heart remain constant in worship before God, regardless of that which is polluted or dying around them.

Often, dear people come to me, troubled at the absence of spiritual vitality in the congregation they attend and speaking of how deeply desirous they are of revival. I understand their hearts and their plights, but my counsel is that they learn from Samuel.

Brokenhearted husbands and wives describe to me the very real pain and agony of their discouraging marital situations, hoping against hope for a change and wondering if some gracious exit is allowable. I care about their pain and understand their concerns. But I always encourage them to try Samuel's style—waiting, growing individually—before they surrender to discouragement or hasten out the doorway of divorce.

Renewal is not something solely needed by churches.

People need renewal.

Marriages need renewal.

Job situations need renewal.

And so do dozens of other human circumstances.

But the flesh is impatient. Revolution, not renewal, is too often its choice. Our flesh wants action, even if it's at the cost of pain. We're inclined to consider this an acceptable trade-off—simply exchanging one kind of pain for another. We are willing to take our lumps in hope that our revolution will secure a new day of God's way. But all too easily we get our way instead, and apparent victory becomes only another kind of defeat. What renewal might have brought with time, revolution demolished in our carnal zeal for speedy results.

The way to avoid this delusion is to wait in worship.

One of the great principles of worship is that it gains dominion not by the force of self-assertion but by the power of praise. Worship wins because the worshiper is willing to sacrifice his comfort and his convenience—and to make room for God to work by His might and in His time.

Samuel's first lesson in renewal is that the childlike, worshiping believer, who keeps renewed from season to

WORSHIP GAINS DOMINION BECAUSE THE WORSHIPER SACRIFICES HIS COMFORT AND CONVENIENCE— AND ALLOWS GOD TO WORK BY HIS MIGHT, IN HIS TIME.

season through a fresh robing of his own soul in the spirit of faith, hope and love, will eventually see renewal. As Hannah did for Samuel, the Holy Spirit will provide ongoing newness if we will allow Him. In the meantime, as Samuel with Eli, we might be disappointed over circumstances that continue without change; we may be weary with those in authority who seem to lack the boldness to effect change where it is needed.

Still, the soul who waits in worship before the throne of God will remain at peace and be fulfilled in the meantime. And he will never be without the confidence that the Lord ultimately is in full control. The old hymn "God Is Still on the Throne" puts it like this:

> God is still on the throne,
>   and He will remember His own.
> Though trials may press us
>   and burdens distress us,
> He never will leave us alone.

> God is still on the throne,
>   He never forsaketh His own.
> His promise is true,
>   He will not forget you;
> God is still on the throne.

Chiding may provoke action and force something that looks like victory, but childlikeness is the only way to ensure that we actually will win.

ICHABOD IS ONLY A NAME

Church traditions might be termed "indeterminately spiritual." That is, a given tradition might be dynamically valid in one setting and not in another. It is not a case of validity (like beauty) being in the eye of the beholder but of true power issuing solely from the hand of God. Thus, if church tradition has lost its contact with God, it becomes a mere formality, for God's touch is no longer on it.

However, it is a mistake to assume that any tradition is devoid of dynamic on the supposition that a present absence of power argues against the tradition itself. Virtually any practice that had once been an avenue of God's visiting in dynamic power is always a potential scene of holy lightning's striking again. It's wise never to mock or mime traditions, because you never know when you may need to see tradition activated for real and holy purposes!

Which brings us to the Ark of the Covenant.

During Samuel's time the ark was the central feature of Israel's worship. It was placed in the holy of holies, the inner sanctum of the Tabernacle, and it contained the Ten Commandments, a commemorative portion of the manna and Aaron's rod that had budded. The whole of it was covered with a small, solid-gold platform called the mercy seat, upon which the blood of atonement was annually presented. If there were any question as to whether this "traditional" box had any power connected to it, the memory still remained in Samuel's time that where the ark was, the presence and power of God had been manifest in the past.

But something had happened—something bad.

As we have already noted, a high priest, whose physical condition seemed to bespeak his spiritual neglect, had proven ineffective at maintaining God's order in his own home. His sons, to whom his priesthood was now being bequeathed, had sorely corrupted their ways and totally ignored the holy standards of the Lord. Although worship *forms* were still being maintained, there was no *power* present. Israel had again become defenseless before her enemies, since God is the only real defense available to any of His people. If they lose their vital touch with Him, they lose touch with the source of all their hope, purpose and power.

The events that followed were a further commentary on the barrenness of spiritual leadership at that time. Eli's sons bear the ark into battle, the Israeli troops are defeated again, the ark is captured by the Philistines, Eli's sons are slain, and he dies from a fall brought on by the shock of hearing the report of such a humiliating defeat and horrible disaster: the Ark of the Covenant . . . lost!

The whole scenario occasioned the naming of a baby—one of the best-known names in the Bible: Ichabod.

Ichabod was Eli's grandson, born prematurely on the day the ark was captured. His mother went into early labor upon hearing of the death of her husband; and although she would die in delivery, she did name the newborn boy: "Call him Ichabod—the glory has departed from Israel!" (see 1 Sam. 4:21).

Chabod is the Hebrew word for glory. It is a word that refers to the idea of weight more than to the "something shiny" we connect with the meaning of "glory." In essence, the idea of glory relates to the substance, the reality of a person, practice or institution. The glory has to do with what it is that causes a thing to excel beyond its counterparts. For Israel, the glory was the presence of the Lord. He was the One who offered them qualities of excellence as a people and powers of excellence in battle. But a battle had been lost, and the dying woman's cry, which labeled her son with a less-than-desired name—Ichabod, or "no glory"—was half right. The glory had departed, but not simply because the ark had been captured. The real weight of God's power in Israel's midst had departed well before.

But Samuel's rising ministry held promise of a recovery.

In studying the life of Samuel, we can learn a few lessons from reviewing this part of his story:

1. We need never fear that the disappearance of God's power and presence from among us will necessarily dilute His purpose or destiny for our lives. Samuel's life and destiny were not hindered or reduced by the sagging spiritual conditions or the disastrous events of that day. He walked with and worshiped God, and God's purpose for him was fulfilled. When we do the same, we will experience the same.

2. Merely sustaining religious forms and formulas argues neither for the presence nor the absence of God's blessing and power. But it is certain that into every situation of spiritual accountability a day of crisis will come. When it does, truth will be verified and sham will be exposed. Neither you nor I need to force the showdown; God will take care of it in His time and by His means.

3. When "Ichabod" is pronounced over a situation, it is important to know that the absent glory does not reveal an absent God. God is never absent, even when the spiritual emptiness of those still exercising once-mighty forms of worship disallows His display of power now.

It is this last point I am most interested in making, for there is an unfortunate habit among spiritually inclined people either to demean traditions or demand too much of them. On the one hand, some are quick to deny the worth of *any* form; on the other, some expect the exercise of religious forms to mandate God's response. The "Ichabod" of God may appear to be branded on a practice, a place or a people, but it is unwise for you or me to say as much. God is often far more present and ready to work than people realize. Don't embarrass yourself by pronouncing the demise of His operations at a place or in a situation where you have given up. Remember this especially when you are tempted to fault those who maintain a firm liturgy in their worship.

It's a mistaken supposition that only high-church or Catholic celebrants conduct a liturgy. A liturgy is any order of service—even the absence of one—or flexibility in order as practiced in the worship of more casual or spontaneous groups. Each of these is an order in its own right. Every liturgy is the fruit of a history lived out by a people who sought God and found Him. The methods of worship they used were invoked at the beginning because they had found something in His Word that sparked their response and thereby shaped their practice. However, as is so often the case given time, forms prevail and purposes become forgotten. The "weight of glory" may thereby be drained from the practice, not because the liturgical practice was useless, but simply because the perfunctory exercise of meaningless motions provides no resting place for the weight of God's glory.

Be assured of this, however: If hungry and thirsty hearts will again search the Word and seek the Lord, an Ichabod spirit cannot prevail. In ancient Israel, God may have refused to bless a sinning people with victory over the Philistines. But when those same Philistines foolishly believe they have added the Lord to their pantheon of deities in Dagon's temple, they soon find out differently. When Samuel rises to worship, God speaks again.

No, the glory of Israel had not departed. God was and is still alive and independently ready to display His power. He's simply searching for those who will meet the conditions.

Enter David.

THE PROMISE OF KINGDOM

Samuel is called the kingmaker because he anointed the first two kings of Israel. He anointed both at God's command—the first, because God permitted the will of the people; the second, because God's will was being done.

Saul is the greatest tragedy of Old Testament history.

He's the country boy who had his chance at greatness, started well, became puffed with pride and turned into a malicious, demon-guided demagogue who, shamed by his enemies, died in battle. David started the same way Saul did: a strapping shepherd boy from the hill country. There is little difference in David's story in terms of its particulars. Both he and Saul won early victories; both were heralded first by part of the people and later by all the people. But there is a radical and central difference in their personalities: David had a heart for God.

In taking lessons in renewal from Samuel, distinguishing between Saul and David is perhaps our most important assignment. You and I may apply the first two lessons drawn from "Sam's Song":

1. We may be wise to wait with patience and walk in worship as God grows His purpose in us, refusing to force the issue of change and awaiting God's time.
2. We may be judicious to remember that the secret of renewal lies not in a particular form or the absence of one, but God's glory waits to visit and fill those who hunger and thirst for Him.

However, if we learn these points well and miss the third, we are in danger of finding the beginning of God's Kingdom power and still miss its continuation. We must be wise at this point, for *continuous* promise and blessing is the objective of God's rule. Historic incidents or sporadic occurrences are no substitute for an "increase of His government and peace which knows no end" (see Isa. 9:7). It is a hard fact that the *appearance* of renewal is far easier to produce than the real thing. And a more demanding truth is this: The actuality of renewal does not guarantee its continuity. Consequently, the seeker after renewal must learn these two disciplines:

1. *Let the Lord give rise to* His *Kingdom demonstration.* Israel's pursuit of a king on their terms brought Saul into the picture. We are no less capable of conjuring up a renewal that looks like God's will and isn't.
2. *Prioritize the heart rather than outward appearances.* This is underscored in God's Word, as Samuel speaks at the anointing of David: "Man looks at the outward appearance, but the LORD looks at the heart" (1 Sam. 16:7).

The maintenance of a right heart requires only that our quest be solely for God and unto His glory. The Lord committed to David that the Messiah would issue from his line and that God would cause that never would there fail to be a king on David's throne. This promise was based on David's heart relationship with God. Sustained blessing always is.

True renewal *comes* where hearts *wait* for God.

True renewal *manifests* where hearts *thirst* for God.

True renewal *stays* where hearts *walk* with God.

Hannah's song set the theme for her son's life: He lifts up . . . He gives strength . . . He exalts (see 1 Sam. 2:7,10). Samuel learned that song and lived out its wisdom. Another learned it from him and made "Sam's Song" the theme of a hundred psalms. He led Israel to a place where her worship brought her to victories unsurpassed in all her history. He learned to link the worship of God with the expansion of His rule through His people. He did both wholeheartedly and victoriously.

His name was David.

CHAPTER 9

BOARDS AND BIG WHEELS WON'T MAKE IT

And to the angel of the church in Philadelphia write, "These things says He who is holy, He who is true, 'He who has the key of David.'"

REVELATION 3:7

It is no coincidence that Israel's greatest development in worship coincided with her broadest boundaries of government.

David was the leader for both.

The one-time shepherd boy who strummed a lyre and sang to his sheep had risen to rule a nation and to teach God's flock to sing His praise. The youthful slayer of Goliath, whose hero-ism and faith stirred an army to boldness, came to the throne and vanquished Israel's enemies.

There is no more insightful study in worship than the life and music of David. In worship he soars; with worship he wars.

The union of the two seems paradoxical, but this king was apparently able to discern God's heart. David knew that God wanted to dwell among His people to bless, to give victory, to shower His mercy and lovingkindness upon them all. David rep-resents the very practical potential in broadening our horizons of worship. He forged a bold union between worship and war-fare, between loving God and wanting His blessing, between exalting the Lord and asking for His help. He bypassed the tra-ditional theological inclinations against such raw requests as bless me, help me, heal me, prosper me.

Many in the Church today consider such direct petitions lacking in spirituality. Ecclesiastical convictions render any hint of "seeking to be blessed" suspect of carnal motivation. Furthermore, the watching, listening, ever-critical citizen of the world scoffs, "If God *does* exist, He's above hearing such mun-dane appeals from mere mortals."

I'm certain David would fall well short of pleasing either of these camps. But God's Word has made another assessment of him entirely:

> When [God] had removed [Saul], He raised up for them
> David as king, to whom also He gave testimony and said,
> "I have found David the son of Jesse, a man after My own
> heart, who will do all My will" (Acts 13:22).

As God Himself confers such a conclusive commendation on David, we can hardly challenge his approach to worship or attribute his applications of it with anything less than nobility. Whatever cheap or shallow misinterpretations of Scripture may today invite believers to charisma without character or to prosperity without propriety, David represented neither imbalance. Yet, David did experience abundance, success and victory upon victory—and worship was at the heart of his movement into such bountiful living and leadership.

But how did it start?

THE SHAPING OF A WORSHIP LEADER

It would be impossible simply from his psalmic references to gain a full understanding of David's discovery of an intimate relationship with God. But he does model intimacy. And with it, emotion.

David exhibits qualities of heart and practices in praise that cannot be shelved or partitioned from our accountability to the truth they reveal. A high view of the Scriptures requires a dual acknowledgment that today's "reformed" worship must face. Two facts—God's testimony to David's understanding of His own heart, and the Holy Spirit's will to include so much of David's worship psalms in the eternal Word—join to force us to deal with these conclusions:

1. God not only is unopposed to emotional worship, He welcomes it.
2. God not only allows the worshiper's plea for success, He rewards it.

There is no evidence that David had a structured agenda for applying these facts, as though he "knew all along that God is like this" or that he thought he could manipulate the Almighty to serve his own private interests. None at all. But there is a clear report in the revelation of God's Word, and there are net results to be totaled. Between these two facts there unfolds the shaping of a man who led his people to worship God at even greater heights.

The public beginning of his leadership in worship took place after David had conquered Jerusalem. His capital city established, he longed to bring back the Ark of the Covenant to a tabernacled center where Israel could again come and seek God. His approach to that mission is most instructive.

THE TABERNACLE OF DAVID

The Tabernacle raised in Moses' time seems to disappear sometime between Joshua and David—an interesting puzzle for Bible students to attempt to solve. After its establishment in Shiloh, following Israel's entry into the land circa 1400 B.C., the Tabernacle is mentioned only four times. After the loss of the Ark of the Covenant to the Philistines during Eli's high priesthood (about 1150 B.C.), it seems that the absence of the very object which made the Tabernacle necessary and which gave reason for its existence, occasioned its virtual demise. During Samuel's ministry he operated from more than one worship center, which apparently confirms that the Tabernacle was probably not in active use.[1]

In the meantime, the Philistines had returned the Ark of the Covenant. After capturing it, they discovered to their dismay that Yahweh was not a dime-store deity to be toyed with or to be added to a pantheon of conquered tribal gods. He was the Lord Jehovah, God of all creation and Israel's Savior. The story of the plague upon their cities and the embarrassment of their god Dagon because of the presence of the Ark of the Covenant would be humorous if it weren't so disastrous to them and so laden with lessons for us (see 1 Sam. 5). For more than 20 years, the ark had been in the village of Kirjath Jearim, where it rested at the household of a man named Abinadab (see 1 Sam. 7:1,2).

At this point we are presented with a story—a series of events that at once reveal David's humanness, his anger and his capacity for misjudgment, as well as his heart for God, his passion for His presence and his humility before the Lord.

DAVID'S HEART FOR GOD

There is a fundamental prerequisite for everyone who would worship God or lead others to do so. David abundantly manifests that quintessential trait of a heart filled with a passion for God:

> My soul thirsts for You; my flesh longs for You in a dry and thirsty land where there is no water. So I have looked for You in the sanctuary, to see Your power and Your glory (Ps. 63:1,2).

David reveals a largeness of heart which not only desires God's working in his own life but also longs for His manifest glory "in the sanctuary." The deep cry of such a leader's soul for both his own need *and* that of his people will never go unrewarded.

So David called the people to join him in a quest: "If it seems good to you, and if it is of the LORD our God . . . let us bring the ark of our God back to us" (1 Chron. 13:2,3).

His objective was to bring the ark to Jerusalem, for David valued the worship of God. He knew the priceless worth of God's presence which always attends those who worship Him, and he prepared a new place for the ark of God to dwell.

Upon the ark's arrival, David conducted a great feast—a magnanimous event which beautifully illustrates that wherever worship is renewed, people will always be both filled with joy and fed. The celebration was also marked by David's introduction of several new songs for the occasion.

We don't know if David led the throng or if he sang the new songs himself. But we do know the music of praise and worship filled the feast time. The book of Chronicles gives us portions of at least three psalms that David had written to the Lord.[2]

All this newness, feasting and rejoicing with high praises to the Lord are the climax to the story. But David managed to bring the ark to Jerusalem only after experiencing considerable difficulty.

DAVID'S HUMANNESS AND ANGER

Why in the world the idea was ever hatched is difficult to decide. The only other time in history that the Ark of the Covenant had been carried on a cart was when the Philistines sent it back, fearful and unwilling even to be near it (see 1 Sam. 6:8,9).

Obviously ignorant or forgetful of the fact that from the time of Moses the Lord had commanded that the ark be carried on the shoulders of the priests, David built a new cart and brought the ark out of the house of Abinadab, whose sons then drove the cart (see 2 Sam. 6:3). The fashioning of the cart is a classic example of man's sincerest efforts proving horribly out of sync with the divine order. David's capacity for human error glares forth here—a rather comforting fact considering the eventual outcome, even though the immediate results were horribly tragic.

The great parade that had been planned to bring the ark to Jerusalem hardly made it out of town. When one of the oxen pulling the cart stumbled, the great gold-covered box started to slide off the cart. Uzzah leaped forward to secure it from falling—and was struck dead! It's a sudden end to a great plan—a tragic conclusion to what had seemed the start of something big. Death seems a bewildering judgment considering all that was being done in a sincere attempt to honor God.

And David became angry.

He named the place *Perez Uzzah*, or "the breach of Uzzah," apparently feeling that a trust he felt he enjoyed with God had been breached. He became afraid, and in his despair he cried out, "How can I bring the ark of God to me?" (1 Chron. 13:12).

THE FASHIONING OF A CART TO CARRY THE ARK IS A CLASSIC EXAMPLE OF MAN'S SINCEREST EFFORTS PROVING HORRIBLY OUT OF SYNC WITH THE DIVINE ORDER.

The ark was parked on the nearest property. The parade ended. Uzzah was buried and David sulked back to Jerusalem, irritated and confused.

* * * * *

I have been so refreshed by the insights on this passage which two fellow pastors shared with me, so let me share their observations. Their words taught me wisdom just at the time I was zealous of seeing a renewal in worship begun with my own people. These pastors' insights into David's worship leadership might help you as much as they helped me.

Don Pickerill observed:

> Look at David building the cart. Can we see ourselves in our dedicated diligence at church work? How many times I've labored on the supposition that God's presence can be brought in on a "new cart"—a new program of some kind. Do you know what carts are made of? *Boards and big wheels!*
>
> Have you ever tried it like I have? If we can just get enough "boards" (teams of people working on the project) and big wheels (a celebrity or successful person here or there), then we can really get things going for God! Oh, how pitiful, Church. Boards and big wheels won't make it. God's presence travels on the shoulders of His priests—that is, on the praises of *all* His people, for *we* are the contemporary "priests of God." He doesn't need our new carts. He simply wants our priestly praise.

Jerry Cook shared his observations on 2 Samuel 6:3,4: "They set the ark of God on a new cart, and brought it out of the house

of Abinadab, which was on the hill; and Uzzah and Ahio, the sons
of Abinadab, drove the new cart. . . . and Ahio went before the ark."

Will you look at the names of the two brothers "helping"
the Ark along—Ahio and Uzzah. I was interested about
this, and looking up the meaning of their names I discovered that Ahio means "friendly" and Uzzah means
"strength." I couldn't help but laugh, because it was so
symbolic of my earliest conceptions of the way ministry
is to succeed; that is, to "roll the old cart along."

First, get an Ahio out in front—you know, somebody
loaded with personality. Mr. Friendly. We seem to think
that what we need to really succeed (I mean *really!*) is to
cultivate a top quality PR approach—public relations.
The closer to Madison Avenue, the better, right?

Then, with PR, we need a backup; we need strength—
people with drive, dynamism and determination. Thus,
what we can't accomplish by skill or personality we'll
compensate for with brute strength. And we try so sincerely—so *very* sincerely—to bring the presence of God
into our churches. And sadly the conclusion is so often
much the same as here. The end of it all is *death*.

The words of both these men sting with the bite of Arctic air
after sitting in a stuffy room. I was alerted and I was counseled
as to exactly why some of my past zeal for God had been so
unproductive.

We who would welcome the presence of God into our
beloved churches would be wise to learn from David's human
error. We may need to repent for the bitterness or angry bewil-
derment we feel because God hasn't blessed our new-cart efforts
of the past with a visitation of His glory.

He is waiting to bless, but humble acceptance of His terms is the only way renewal can be realized.

DAVID'S HUMILITY BEFORE GOD

Few things are more difficult to do than to admit when we are wrong. It isn't so much our unwillingness to acknowledge failures or mistakes but our fear that if we do so, no one will remember that we *meant* well even though we didn't *do* well.

David was willing to be wrong and to start over.

After three months, a report reached him: The farmland of Obed-Edom, where the ark had been left when Uzzah died, was being blessed with great fruitfulness. The message was clear: The problem wasn't that God didn't want to bless his efforts; the problem was with not knowing how to receive His blessing.

Because of this report, David consulted Zadok and Abiathar, the leading priests. They explained to him the proper order for transporting the ark. The pattern had apparently been overlooked because the Tabernacle was in disuse and it had been so long since the priestly ministry had been exercised in moving the ark. Zadok and Abiathar had searched the scrolls and discovered that the ark must be borne on the shoulders of the priests (see 1 Chron. 15:2,15).

The issue is painfully clear—painful to the point of Uzzah's death and David's frustration. God doesn't need pushing; He calls for praise. God doesn't use programs; He uses people—people who worship Him!

The ensuing scene described in 2 Samuel 6:12-15 is aglow with a combination of new wisdom in worship and new rejoicing through praise:

- Instead of percussion and stringed instruments as at the first attempt to move the ark, the silver breath of trumpet sound fills the air. (Could this contain a message on the difference between the work of our flesh and the breath of the Spirit?)
- Instead of carnal efforts at securing God's reputation—Uzzah's attempt to balance the ark—sacrifices are offered at regular intervals all the way to Jerusalem, fulfilling God's Word.
- Instead of a vocally silent entourage, praiseless except for the musicians' best efforts and the accompanying hoofbeats of oxen, this time the instrumental music is joined by the throng's raising their voices with resounding joy!

Human concern for retaining an air of sophistication has been cast aside. And as though to conclusively verify the childlike passion and purity of motive compelling his whole pursuit of God's glory and his delight over anticipating broader blessing, David suddenly breaks into a dance.

It was not a casual affair.

The king himself, usually garbed in regal clothing befitting his office, lays aside his outer garments and begins to dance. We are not told the duration of his dancing, its tempo or its style. But we do know that David was specifically rejoicing in the dance as an act of humility before God. He was ecstatic, to be sure, but he hadn't lost his mind. He had found the presence of God!

And thus the ark came to Jerusalem.

Listen! The dancer seems to be singing as he leads the way to a new Tabernacle which he has prepared to receive the heavenly Visitor:

Praise is awaiting You, O God, in Zion;
And to You the vow shall be performed.
O You who hear prayer,
To You all flesh will come (Ps. 65:1).

Feasting will follow. Israel's boundaries will continue to enlarge. Worship will be learned at dimensions yet unknown among the people, for a leader of worship is the leader of the people.

His heart for God is single, his human misjudgments dealt with, his humility before God a model for his people.

But there is one problem that David will face before nightfall: There are always people who resist worship, because its price involves new and renewing lessons in humility.

There is always a Michal.

CHAPTER 10

DANCING KINGS
AND BARREN QUEENS

Once told at Yale is the story of a Harvard cheerleader who, impeccably
dressed in tie and tans, arose to lead a yell, saying in a beautifully modulated
voice, "Come, deah students, let us give three cheeahs foah deah old Hahvad—
not so loud as to be boisterous but sufficient to demonstrate ouah enthusiasm!"

Michal was infuriated.

Her husband's partial disrobing before all his subjects, when
he stripped his royal outer garment to allow freedom for dancing his praise to the Lord God of Israel, was in her opinion inex-
cusable. The spectacle had been executed with his actually wear-
ing a light linen ephod—only a humble priestly smock instead of

apparel befitting his high office. She complained: "How glorious was the king of Israel today, uncovering himself today in the eyes of the maids of his servants, as one of the base fellows shamelessly uncovers himself!" (2 Sam. 6:20). An uninformed listener would have thought David guilty of exhibitionism—of stark nudity and an obscene display. But he had only danced in joyous praise to God.

Michal had watched it from the window of their home as the procession drew near Jerusalem, toward the Tabernacle her husband had erected to welcome the ark of God's covenant. And look! With all the people watching, David was "leaping and whirling before the LORD," and as she watched, Michal "despised him in her heart" (2 Sam. 6:16). Upon the king's arrival home that evening his wife unloaded on him. And so she faced another kind of music—barrenness.

The sum of this story spells out a tale that has been told over and over again, and one that today's reformation in worship demands be told once more. It's a message full of wisdom and warning—not a warning of impending divine judgment, but one of wisdom as to the implications of pride. It's a warning of what can happen when human tastes reject the childlike simplicity and practical humility at worship that pleases the divine.

Barren. Childless. Unfruitful and unproductive.

They all describe Michal from that encounter forward. Though she was married to the king, from the day she so scathingly assaulted her husband's worship, she "had no children to the day of her death" (2 Sam. 6:23). We aren't told if David rejected any conjugal relationship or if it was a curse that somehow came upon her. But David had responded to her charges:

[My dancing] was before the LORD, who chose me instead of your father and all his house, to appoint me ruler over the people of the LORD, over Israel. Therefore I will play music before the LORD. And I will be even more undignified than this, and will be humble in my own sight (2 Sam. 6:21,22).

One would have thought her heritage would have recommended more wisdom than Michal showed. She was daughter to the deposed King Saul. Her father had not only lost his throne but before his death had also shown hideous and unjustified jealousy and hatred toward David, who was guilty only of being a faithful warrior. Now with Saul's entire house overthrown by his own folly and defeat, his daughter Michal might well have suffered capital punishment as the remnant of a family known to be hostile to David. Yet David continues to show mercy by sparing her life. Michal will live, but she will live a cardboard existence, bereft of all the joys that might have been.

MY MAJESTY IN THE MIRROR

I have grown unable to read that story without being reminded of our human preoccupation with dignity and of a brutal confrontation God brought me to with this problem in my own heart. Allow me to relate a personal story.

One is hard put at times to know the best way to tell of personal encounters with the Lord. To many people, the mere suggestion of someone's saying "The Lord spoke to me" is roughly equivalent to claiming they had tea that afternoon on the planet Venus with alien beings. To others, opinions about the relative validity of such a report vary—from the notion that the entire conversation was concocted, to the cautious venturing of the possibility that God just *might* have spoken.

To whatever category my testimony may relegate me in your estimation, I cannot describe one of my most important experiences in Christ without telling you it began with a specific set of words from Him—just three words, following which neither the Lord nor I spoke. I did argue, debating mentally in my best forensic style as I recoiled from what He had spoken. But each argument was instantly deflated by so irrefutable a rebuttal that my debate was silenced. It wasn't He who returned my argument. Simple honesty had me cornered. I simply and intuitively knew that to remain honest with God's dealings in my own heart, I had to obey the command of that quiet internal voice I recognized so well.

"Dance for me," the voice said.

That's right. God told me to dance.

I had been at prayer for an extended period of time one morning, using the church sanctuary as my prayer room. No one was there, except for staff people in several of the offices. You can possibly appreciate my dilemma. Even if I did respond to the voice and perform some holy jig—after all, who can say no to God?!—there was a good chance it would not remain just between Him and me. I felt I certainly didn't need someone to step in and witness the pastor cavorting about like a rank fanatic!

It's difficult to summarize the thoughts racing through my mind as I futilely attempted to negotiate the situation with the Most High. I could instantly think of innumerable reasons for not dancing: It was impractical, unnecessary, undesirable and entirely unreasonable! And yet none of the reasons was convincing, because deep down I knew the *real* issue. What God was dealing with was not dancing but my dignity—*false* dignity. Raw, carnal, fear-filled, self-centered *pride*.

I was the victim of Michal's Syndrome—that not-so-rare affliction that characterizes those of us who are more preoccupied with our style, sophistication or dignity than we are with being childlike in praising God.

Michal's Syndrome is subject to a wide variety of "expert" opinions. Like competing physicians trying to be first to identify a new virus, there are religious analysts who hasten to advance their varied opinions lest a contagion of simplicity rampage through the Church. Their opinions span the spectrum of tastes so much so that if you simply, frankly, flatly don't want expressive worship, you can always find a spiritual expert whose second opinion will justify yours:

- "Well, some people just *need* a lot of exuberance. Others of us don't." (The implication is that *mature* people don't.)
- "It's all a matter of a person's cultural background. You and I are culturally reserved." (The implication is that "reserved" is socially superior or culturally advanced.)
- "You must watch out for emotionalism; it becomes so subjective and worship loses its objectivity in worshiping God and starts to center on man." (The theological concern for God's glory obviously makes this righteously unchallengeable.)
- "I believe—don't you?—that everyone should worship God in his own way and according to his own beliefs. After all, to do otherwise is . . . well, it's . . . it's uncivil." (You know, each of us should worship God according to the dictates of his own heart.)
- (Smiling smugly) "I wouldn't let it worry me. After all, what difference can it make? God looks on the heart, anyway. All this activity doesn't add a thing!" (The ease with which the leader/counselor/observer dismisses this issue as irrelevant consoles our quest for an escape from accountability as to our own responsiveness.)

The issue is expressiveness—openness, forthrightness, any assertive display of praise in worship settings beyond socially acceptable, cooperative singing. It begets a bevy of opinions from wild support to angered resistance. It has made me nervous many times, too.

Several of the above arguments had registered with me over the years, and I could think of others. Having had a broad mixture of church background, running the gamut from Presbyterianism and Methodism to Pentecostalism, I knew the do's and don'ts of every circle in evangelical Christianity. When it came to acceptable and unacceptable worship practices, I knew dancing wasn't one that any of them smiled on. So I didn't like the idea at all, and I felt that God Himself was bullying me to the wall on an issue we all had the right to differ over.

I had my theology to stand upon, too.

After all, I knew as I stood there—"Dance for me" still reverberating through my brain—that God's acceptance of me wasn't based on my antics at praise. I knew He doesn't measure anyone by a set of calisthenics! But just as all these thoughts ran through my mind, I became aware of one stark fact: I could win this argument with myself, but I would risk losing something with God. I recognized that my potential "loss" was a hard lesson in humility—

in remaining as a child before the Father,

in keeping small in my own eyes,

in refusing the encrustation of religious sophistry which can inevitably calcify the bones of anyone's soul and grip him with a spiritual arthritis.

So, I danced.

I didn't do it well, but then, only God was looking. And within my heart I felt the warm, contented witness that my Abba Father was pleased.

I knew His pleasure wasn't because He had won an argument but because I had won a victory. I knew He wasn't happy because He had managed to exploit my vulnerability but because I had chosen to *remain* vulnerable. I knew He wasn't dangling me as a puppet-like toy because He needed my dancing but because I needed to respond that way. He knew it was essential to ensure my future flexibility and my availability for learning the pathway of worship-unto-fruitfulness.

That last point is so important—fruitfulness. Because the Michal Syndrome can lead anyone to a rationalized sense of superiority, it can come at the expense of a deadly, spiritual fruitlessness. Barrenness is a high price to pay for one's dignity.

That was one classic encounter with my own pride, of seeing "*my* majesty in the mirror," of coming to terms with the horrifying power of self-consciousness, of fear and pride to marshal their forces and successfully plead for their survival. But seeing those liars parading as "my majesty," I determined to bow to *His* Majesty instead.

I share that testimony at my own expense—and very much at the risk of sounding either disgustingly fanatical or impractically mystical. But I relate it in order to help us hear more than my description of a moment's dance of death-to-pride. Rather, I invite our discussion of one of the biblical facts about worship—an issue that seems inevitably to become a battleground.

Expressiveness.

Bold, lively, joyous congregational singing.

Spoken, spontaneous praises amid the congregation.

Shouts of "Hallelujah!" or "Praise the Lord!"

Upraised hands stretched forth in worship.

Clapping of hands, in tempo with the music or as applause expressed to God.

The list could go on, but the essence of the problem is on the table. We are at a great watershed point of Christian worship—and fellowship. There are strong opinions, deep emotions and intense boundary lines drawn on this theme; and to espouse an open, free response is to invite accusations: Confusion! Disorder! Charismatic! Emotionalism!

But before conclusions or accusations of silly or sectarian practices increase, maybe it would be better to look into the Word of God. In doing so, David is a good point of reference, for in him we have a beautiful blend of (1) someone whose *heart* attitude is attested to *by* God and (2) someone whose *humility* was verified *before* God. With his combination of character and childlikeness, and with the evidence of the Word that flowed through his pen, we have a solid source of guidance toward acceptable worship.

NEW TESTAMENT WORSHIP

Peculiarly, David presents us with a very *New* Testament worship model. Though he lived a millennium before Christ, David's directives concerning worship in its form and practice greatly influenced the worship of the first-century Church, inasmuch as the Old Testament was all the Bible they had.

Opponents of expressive worship will occasionally concede that the New Testament does contain a few references to forthright, open praise. Still, the presumption is that expressiveness in worship went out with the blood-sacrifice system or that such unabashed physical exuberance was only a cultural trait passed down by Hebrew tradition. It's as though the apostles dispensed with open, enthusiastic praise at the same time they did away with actual circumcision!

But the essence of sacrifice has never left worship, and it never will:

Therefore by Him let us continually offer the sacrifice of praise to God, that is, the fruit of our lips, giving thanks to His name (Heb. 13:15).

As to writing off biblical expressiveness as an ancient cultural trait, we must wrestle with the question of God's Word and its authority to command our behavior regardless of our cultural environment. Any resistance I may naturally feel toward open, expressive worship is not justified on an appeal to my culture. The tendency of man has *always* been against the sacrifice of our own ways and against surrender to His. The willfulness of my human nature mandates that the Bible must remain the arbiter of my tastes, not my culture.

So let's look at the Word together. First of all, the New Testament contains more direct references to expressive worship than usually meet the eye. Singing, praising, upraised voices, lifted

WORSHIP IN SPIRIT AND TRUTH INVOLVES THE TOTAL HUMAN BEING— SPIRIT, MIND, EMOTIONS AND BODY.

hands, kneeling, offerings and reading of the Scriptures are all mentioned.[1] Even though these examples of expressive worship are not more frequently mentioned in current books and discussion on the topic, this does not eliminate the fact that New Testament worship was full spectrum.

Every believer possesses the wisdom to recognize that worship is not a single-dimensional exercise of the human personality. Worship is certainly not a cerebral pursuit, some sort of mystical consciousness or an emotional binge, although it does involve reason, spiritual intuition and emotions. According to the Scriptures, worship "in spirit and truth" (John 4:23) involves the total human being—spirit, mind, emotions and body.

Paul registered a clear-cut appeal for this order of worship. The following paraphrase of Romans 12:1,2 (with parenthetical commentary) underscores the multidimensional nature of New Testament worship and the requirement that we go beyond mere human reasoning to *enter in* and participate:

> Therefore, I appeal to you brothers (an emotional call based on the preceding revelation in chapters 1—11), as you witnessed and experienced God's mercies (a further expression reaching to touch the heart), that you bring before Him a sacrifice of worship fully alive at every dimension—involving your body (physical), your mind (intellectual) and your Spirit (spiritual). This is wholly acceptable as a sacrifice and is the most intelligent and spiritual worship possible. To achieve this you must break free of the world-mind and allow the Spirit to transform your thinking in order that you may discover the full counsel of God's will.[2]

The New Testament worshiper is, of course, beyond the era of blood sacrifice, for there is no longer any requirement of sacrifices for sin. Christ has fulfilled all such requirements as our Savior, the Lamb of God. But David foresaw our day and described in song the timeless spirit of sacrifice that would ever and always be essential when worship is offered to the Living God:

> For You do not desire sacrifice,
> or else I would give it;
> You do not delight in burnt offering.
> The sacrifices of God are a broken spirit,
> A broken and contrite heart—
> These, O God, You will not despise
> (Ps. 51:16,17).

Such sacrifices *are* physical and they *do* require humility. The basic meaning of *proskuneo*, the New Testament Greek word for worship, corresponds to *shawkhaw*, the Old Testament Hebrew term. Both mean to prostrate oneself, or to stetch out with face on the ground in adoration or submission. While it is possible to actually do this in a private time of devotion, the act of lying facedown on the carpet is neither practical nor required—nor is it generally recommended—when believers are gathered in assembly.

Nevertheless, there is a prostrating that ought *always* to be required: the prostrating of pride and the flattening of the human will, which so readily inclines to assert its own dignity at the expense of humble participation in full-hearted, spiritually alive and physically expressed worship.

BODY LANGUAGE

Michal objected to David's physical expressiveness in worship. He might have marched sedately, sung discreetly or thought

noble thoughts interminably—but sparks flew when he danced!
They still do.

People still become upset when physical or verbal expressiveness exceeds their learned limits, and one can find in the Scriptures excess or tastelessness that cannot be rationalized. But the irony of our reaction to excess is that we race toward the other extreme.

If someone shrieks aloud in a fanatical (possibly demonic) display, grossly interrupting a service where new expressiveness is being attempted, the likelihood is that the countermove will be a virtual full retreat—an immediate return to cold reserve and the safety of relative silence. And not just now but from now on. The dummies and the demons win. The sincere are silenced, as it seems the only perceived security against fanatical intrusion or noisy extremism is an equally ridiculous *nothing*.

So it is that verbal praising has become taboo in some circles, and understandably so, given the bizarre cases of the never actually seen but oft-reported ("we've heard that . . .") stereotypes which spook people from trying. The same goes for upraised hands or clapping. It only takes one or two people in a group who flail their arms mindlessly during every song or who become clap-happy at the drop of a phrase from the pulpit. A single stupid display can reduce an entire congregation to absolute unwillingness to attempt what otherwise are very biblical expressions of praise and worship.

It would be best to leave this dilemma alone if it weren't for the fact that the issue touches at the core of my point. You see, it is precisely at this point—open public expressiveness—that our will to humble ourselves is most delicately touched. The inclination to preserve my dignity or to reserve "my right to not participate" is confronted by such directives in the Word as:

Oh, clap your hands, all you peoples! Shout to God with the voice of triumph! For the LORD Most High is awesome; He is a great King over all the earth (Ps. 47:1,2).

But sufficient internal and external reasons, as I've elaborated, survive to provide fully justifiable excuses for my not responding to God's Word when it exhorts: Clap! Shout!

There is an inescapable sanity to the body language of applause at appropriate points in worship. The command calls for such praise on the basis of our Lord's triumphant victory. This should overcome any reserve we might have on the supposition that such expressiveness is superficial. Have you ever heard someone say that people who applaud in church are not regarding God with sufficient reverence? It may possibly be true that some are not. But even if that were so, their shallowness does not justify my indifference to the biblical command.

We are capable of employing an eerie kind of pride that excuses us from responsiveness because we feel someone else may be responding without the depth of understanding we feel we have. We can only nurse such false reasoning if we are willing to violate two other commands: (1) not to judge others whose hearts we cannot see and (2) to present our bodies as forthright worshipers.

The Scriptures call us to glorify God with high praises when you and I gather with the Church:

Let them exalt Him also in the assembly of the people (Ps. 107:32).

I will give You thanks in the great assembly; I will praise You among many people (Ps. 35:18).

Make a joyful noise unto the LORD, all the earth: make a loud noise, and rejoice, and sing praise (Ps. 98:4, *KJV*).

Of course, "noise" isn't the object. Mere noisiness is never a virtue. It is unfortunate, however, that reverence has come to be considered synonymous with silence or, at least, as a reserved quietness. To the contrary, there are some situations in which the least appropriate response is a reserved silence. The celebration of God's lovingkindness, the manifestation of His power, the testimony of His faithfulness—all may inspire praiseful expressiveness.

Blessed are the people who know the joyful sound! They walk, O LORD, in the light of Your countenance (Ps. 89:15).

That joyful sound may be applause, laughter, praise or triumphant song, but it can only sound forth from a liberated, sensitive worshiper. David's example urges us toward being both, and it is possible to experience the release of that joy when discreet leadership and a responsive congregation join heart and hands to do so with balance and beauty.

THE CONGREGATION AS A CHOIR

It is the uniting of a congregation—an assembled *body* of worshipers—which allows for the most beautiful and dynamic *body language*. A confidence and freedom comes when a group has moved beyond being a miscellaneous assortment of worshipers to become a cohesive, worshipful body. As long as expressiveness is merely tolerated and widely scattered, participation will always remain sporadic and at the whim of individual worshipers, and the congregation will never discover real freedom. The quest for both liberty and unity requires that the leadership teach, define and direct. This begins by distinguishing between individuality and spontaneity.

Individuality can be whimsical, disordered or counterproductive because it prevents real unity in congregational worship. But spontaneity is not whimsical; it's responsive. And a whole congregation can be led together in spontaneous responsiveness.

Let me elaborate.

Because there are so many verses in the Bible showing more expressiveness than we generally practice in the Church today, an honest reading of Scripture leads many earnest, hungry worshipers to inquire, "How can *we* do this?"

Their "How?" is not so much a question of form as it is "How can this be done in a decent and orderly way?" Of course, that's also a scriptural concern, for all things are to be done that way. (The Greek text of 1 Corinthians 14:40 is literally rendered "in a gracious and charming way.") How can such specific practices as upraised hands, clapping or concerted verbal praise be "in order" or, for that matter, "decent"?

Having led worship and observed its practice among many different traditions, I believe that what confounds the possibility of fullest release are false ideas about the supposed righteousness of individuality, i.e., *anyone* doing *anything, anytime* he feels like it. For some, complete independence is their sole definition of liberty. For them, submission to headship means surrender to manipulation, and they see agreed cooperation with a whole congregation as a sacrifice of their liberty. But honesty with experience reveals that when such a spirit prevails, the only "free" person in the worship service will be the one "taking liberty."

The rest of the assembly become bound—bound to endure whatever the "liberated" member does, inasmuch as his individuality holds them at his mercy.

Because I longed to see our congregation move toward unity in an expressive, childlike, humble and spiritually sensitive approach to worship, I knew we would have to deal with historic false notions about individuality. To circumvent that takeover spirit of "do-my-own-thing-ism"—which is nothing more than a tyrannical lack of consideration of others—I introduced the concept of the congregation as a choir.

It doesn't take a great mind to understand that a choir could never function in either beauty or worshipfulness if its members operated independently of one another. People can easily see the incongruity of a choir's functioning in any other way than together, if we demonstrate illustrations of the point. It can provide for considerable humor and greatly strengthen the point!

Togetherness was at the heart of the apostle Paul's appeal to the congregation in Corinth: "Brethren, *when you come together. . .*" (1 Cor. 11:33, emphasis mine). His whole purpose in chapter 14 of his first letter to the Corinthians is not to remove liberty but to call for it by teaching people the idea of order—orchestration in worship without suffocation in spirit. He directed them to an order that removed the confusion that had evolved from unwise, impulsive practices by individuals in the assembly. Their sincerity wasn't in question, but the relative wisdom of such independent behavior was.

The agreement of a congregation to move together as a choir, under the direction of their worship leader or pastor, is not a surrender to manipulation or mindless participation. It is an entry into unity and into a genuine liberty that becomes dynamic as sincere worshipers participate together in praise, in song, in upraised hands, in applause or in a concerted shout. "Hallelujah!"

THE PATH OF PRAISE

David taught Israel to worship at new levels—from new songs to new instruments to new demonstrations of praise. There is something about David's leading the people to a new Tabernacle that has deep meaning for us today. In Acts 15, when the leaders of the Early Church gathered to determine in council to what degree Gentile converts would be required to maintain Old Testament ordinances, James addressed the situation with a quotation from the prophet Amos:

> After this I will return and will rebuild the tabernacle of David, which has fallen down; I will rebuild its ruins, and I will set it up; so that the rest of mankind may seek the LORD, even all the Gentiles who are called by My name, says the LORD who does all these things (Acts 15:16).

James's insight applied the text from Amos 9:11,12 to help solve the question they faced then, but interestingly that same passage has another application for us today. James's focus was on all mankind flowing together in the worship of God; our focus is on the worship itself. It excites the imagination to see that this prophecy of God's last-days gathering of the nations includes a prophecy of a last-days rebuilding of the Tabernacle of David!

David's Tabernacle was, in his time, more than a renewal; it was a reformation. There was an adjustment forward and newness everywhere. Prevailing above it all was a humble, childlike spirit of praise that paved the path to fruitfulness, joy and victory. David's expressiveness was at the heart of this breakthrough, just as Michal's resistance was at its throat. But as surely as we may avoid Michal's Syndrome and its consequent barrenness, we can enter into the new reformation. A willingness to accept David's heart attitude *and* childlike exuberance in praise may bring us to a local "rebuilding" of David's Tabernacle. This holds such high promise of real rejoicing and abounding fruit. It is worth moving toward the formation of a congregation who learns to worship as a choir—singing unto the Lord a new song, praising in unity, humbly coming into God's presence with freed expressiveness and thanksgiving.

The reward of worship is God's enthroned presence.

David sang, "But You are holy, enthroned in the praises of Israel." This oft-quoted statement from Psalm 22:3 deserves our greatest understanding, since the implications of the verb *yawshab* are dramatic. Though the basic idea of the word is to sit down, when the King of the universe is the subject it is appropriately translated "enthroned." This great truth resounds to every generation: *Praise creates a dwelling place for God in man's present situation!*

David is not saying that praise makes God bigger or more powerful. Nonsense! Nor is he saying that praise forces God to take any particular action—He is Sovereign! But the text does say: When you praise God—whatever the situation—you can count on Him to move into the middle of it! Thus it is understandable why a worshiping, praising congregation is so desirable an entity:

- It is satisfying to God, who is seeking those who will worship Him in spirit and in truth.

- It is fulfilling to those who worship, for God visits them in blessing and in power.
- It is inspiring to those who enter into such a setting, even though they may be new to it.

People will recognize God's presence and they will respond to it, for there are few human beings who do not deeply, honestly hunger for a vital touch from the Fountain of their being.

My deep desire for the continued prospect of His presence is what led me to remind our congregation of the strong promptings to praise we have received as the Holy Spirit of exhortation has operated among us.

That praise has been a hallmark of our corporate life at The Church On The Way is known to all; that it is a generally accepted practice in our midst is very clear. But praise must remain eminent in our understanding and participation. Over the years some lovely truths have been welded together as the Spirit has brought edification and comfort. Here is the gist of some basic messages that have been delivered to us:

1. The darkness surrounds this hour as it did Paul and Silas in the Philippian prison. Their praise brought God's hand by an earthquake and out of the night a hopeless jailer was saved. Now, let your praises rise. As you praise continually, spiritual shock waves go out into the world around you. Continuous praise will bring your release and the release of many into the kingdom of God (see Acts 16:19-34).

2. Praise is your pathway through the mired circumstances of the present world. Your step will be uncertain and your foot will slide unless you recognize that your praises form stepping-stones by which the Father

paves your way into the future purpose He has for you
(see Ps. 26).

3. "As the morning stars sang My praise at creation," says
   God, "accompanying My great display of power with
   their worship, let your voices join with the heavenly
   song." Praise the Lord. Sing unto the Lord. Sing with
   your spirit and sing with your understanding. For as
   you sing praises unto Him, He continues His great creative working. And in your midst you shall see the
   marvelous works of God, the Lord of the new creation
   (see Job 38:4-7).

* * * * *

I once heard someone say, "'Let's just praise the Lord' is a rather
closed view of things." I understood their meaning, for they had
come from a circle of folks who neither praised the Lord with
understanding, as the psalmist commands, nor did they have a
corporate "Forward, march!" mentality like the one David and
his people manifested. One is forced to agree that praise for
praise's sake can become a wearying experience in redundancy
and pointlessness.

But there is a path of praise that leads to life, and many are
moving forward on it with great joy, growth and renewal. David
walked that path and, in childlike abandon, broke into leaping
and dancing. His humility of heart brought a ready response to
the Holy Spirit of joy motivating him; and even though Michal
protested, David's Tabernacle was built, it housed the ark, and it
was filled with the praises of the Lord.

I vote to help build it again!

CHAPTER 11

THE LIFE-BEGETTING POWER OF SONG

Sing, O barren, you who have not borne! Break forth into singing. . . . For you shall expand to the right and to the left, and your descendants will inherit the nations.

ISAIAH 54:1-3

She was the picture of shyness, standing at the door and bashfully glancing my way, with one finger curled to her lower lip and her eyes eloquently inquiring, *Can I see you, Pastor Jack?*

I beckoned to her, and the eight-year-old walked across the prayer room to where I stood with some elders. Though the service was about to begin, I knelt to greet the child, so our eyes were at the same level.

"Hi, Aimee," I smiled. "What do you want?"

She was so sweetly childlike. "Pastor Jack, I wanted you to hear a song the Lord gave to me."

The service was imminent, but right then she seemed a more precious and urgent matter than the multitude gathering for worship.

"Sing it for me," I said. And she did.

It was a tender little tune. The child's loving lyric voiced her worship and gave expression to first discoveries in the Holy Spirit's creativity in song.

"That's beautiful, Aimee. You keep singing it to the Lord Jesus, will you?"

She nodded and we hugged each other as I whispered, "Thank you for coming to share your song with me. Tell Mama and Daddy hello for me, and . . . ," I paused and then added, "I love you."

Her smile would have melted a million hearts as she said, "I love you, too," and then slipped out the door and hurried to wherever her mom and dad were seated.

There's more to Aimee's story, but for the moment I pause to underscore a conviction about worship and song: *God wants to give everyone his or her own song of praise to Him.*

The Creator, whose Word repeatedly says, "Sing unto the Lord a new song," wants to beget a new song on the lips and from the hearts of His own—a distinctly new song of *your* own! This is not to suggest that everybody's "new song" is appropriate for everyone else or that they should supplant those we've learned together.

But my response to Aimee's song was more than a pastor's kindness to a child; it was my confirmation of a vital practice. She had never heard me encourage private song making in worship, but at her tender age she was experiencing a creative possi-

THE LIFE-BEGETTING POWER OF SONG 163

bility open to us all. While we are not all composers, able to refine melody and lyric, we all have the potential to sing songs spontaneously to the Lord.

THE FULL SPECTRUM OF SONG

Worship may be possible without song, but nothing contributes more to its beauty, majesty, dignity and nobility or to its tenderness and intimacy. There is a full spectrum of purposes and practices of song in worship. The breadth of style, the endless melodic possibilities, the delicate nuances of choral dynamics, the brilliant luster of instrumental arrangement, the soul-stirring anthems of anointed choirs, the rumbling magnificence of giant organs—all seem clearly to be God-given means for our endless expansion and creativity in worship. New musical expression is fitting as we each discover new things about the manifold wisdom of the Lord our God.

God's Word is full of the music of worship from creation to Revelation, and while songs of praise existed long before his time, it's to David we usually turn in learning of song from the Scriptures. The shepherd-boy-turned-mighty-king apparently cultivated the use of song in praise to a dimension previously unexplored.

After raising the Tabernacle in Jerusalem and anticipating the building of the Temple, David organized and provided for the support of music leaders and ministries to enhance Israel's worship (see 1 Chron. 25:2-7). Choirs and orchestras not only were prepared to sing and play skillfully, but they also were selected for their sensitivity to the spirit of prophecy. The careful detail in the specific listing of names tells us something of the importance given to music under David's role:

> [They] prophesied with a harp to give thanks and to
> praise the LORD. All these were under the direction of
> their father for the music in the house of the LORD. . . .
> with their brethren who were instructed in the songs of
> the LORD (1 Chron. 25:3,6,7).

This description reveals a blend both of spontaneity to the Holy Spirit and preparedness for skilled musical presentation. Their prophesying involved more than setting existing Scripture to music. These musicians were to wait on the Lord for inspiration—living truth that would ignite worship and joy in the hearts of God's people. But diligence to duty was not neglected in the name of mysticism. They were instructed in the Lord's song in two ways: (1) in their work on instruments and voice and (2) in their waiting on the Spirit of God.

Beyond providing insights into the obvious value of organizing church music leadership, David's emphasis on and approach to worship issues a summons to awakening and advancement. Moses longed for the day that all of God's people would prophesy (see Num. 11:29); shouldn't we also expect our choirs and instruments to minister with the gift of prophecy? Isn't it possible that the New Testament restoration of the Tabernacle of David may bring us to new dimensions of Holy Spirit-inspired praise and worship in song?

There is a lovely balance in David's institution of musically skilled and spiritually anointed worship. His blend of order and flexibility is not easily attained in any era, but his approach deserves a fresh welcome in today's Church. What guidelines does the New Testament offer us for expecting and cultivating music in corporate and personal worship?

It is extremely significant that the apostle Paul twice issues explicit directives to sing psalms, hymns and spiritual songs. He makes it abundantly clear that the purpose for this is to do more than belt out religious tunes, odes and ditties; in fact, song fuels spiritual growth: "Let the word of Christ dwell in you richly . . . singing" (Col. 3:16), and "Do not be drunk with wine, in which is dissipation; but be filled with the Spirit . . . singing" (Eph. 5:18,19). The first of these edicts establishes a direct relationship between the Word and worship, while the second calls for the Spirit in worship.

A closer look at these verses not only establishes the value of music in New Testament worship, but a new area is opened in worship as well—something we might expect under the new covenant:

> Let the word of Christ dwell in you richly in all wisdom, teaching and admonishing one another in psalms and hymns and spiritual songs, singing with grace in your hearts to the Lord (Col. 3:16).

Here, the fruitful implanting of the Word of God is linked to our singing and worshiping. Most of us would think of these as separate operations—the Word as instructional and song as inspirational. But instead, human intellect and emotion are integrated *through* song, and effective teaching is said to require worship for its fullest accomplishment. The complement of worshipful song is needed for the meat of the Word to be assimilated into our character and conduct. Just as our digestive systems process food and distribute nutrients throughout the body, so worshipful singing is apparently essential for the integration of the Word into our lives.

Could the music of worship be the means God has ordained for fulfilling the covenant made long ago?

But this is the covenant that I will make . . . I will put My law in their minds, and write it on their hearts (Jer. 31:33).

I will put My Spirit within you and cause you to walk in My statutes, and you will keep My judgments and do them (Ezek. 36:27).

Perhaps it's true that Spirit-filled worship is the distinct means by which the new covenant transcends the old in terms of the Word in our lives. No longer is the Word engraved on stone or confined to parchment, but its precepts are being infused into the human personality. Recognizing the place of song in this process certainly reveals the priority of worship. Our singing becomes infinitely more than droning out another ode to orthodoxy. Worshipful singing expedites a process that quickens our minds to receive the Word and submits our souls to the Holy Spirit's implanting it within us. Spirit-filled worship may be our insurance against merely learning facts from the Bible instead of receiving power through its teaching.

In this light, Paul's second mention of singing becomes all the more meaningful. First, two direct commands stand in stark juxtaposition: Don't be unwise. Do know God's will! (see Eph. 5:17). Then follows the call to sing:

Don't be drunk with wine, it only dissipates you; rather, keep on being refilled with the Holy Spirit, a path practiced best by continued singing among yourself of psalms, hymns and spiritual songs (Eph. 5:18,19, author's paraphrase).

There is no mystery to the message here: If you want to walk in God's will and wisdom, avoid the world's spirits and keep filled with God's Spirit—song-filled worship is the way to do both!

Any notion that music is extracurricular is destroyed in Paul's directives. Worship is presented as essential to growth, wisdom, understanding and godly fruitfulness. Word-centeredness and Spirit-fullness are joined at the altar of songful worship, and this balance confronts anyone's temptation to sacrifice either since both are made interdependent.

So clear an assignment and such potential fruit mandate our familiarity with "psalms, hymns and spiritual songs." What are they and how can we apply them in worship?

Singing Psalms

The New Testament Church—Jew and Gentile alike—accepted and used the worship literature of the Old Testament. The Scriptures were viewed as God's inspired Word, and worship from this source was first and foremost. Singing psalms was not only to sing the words of the text but also to sing the inspired utterances of God! Psalm singing was known to be God-glorifying and life-instilling because God's Word was being breathed into the heart as it was breathed out in song.

Today's psalm singing is reflected in those songs that are essentially Scripture set to music. The new reformation has sparked more singing of God's Word in the last 20 years than perhaps at any earlier time in Church history. Yet while this has been happening, a strange, fearful questioning or resistance to this development is occasionally found.

A pastor who had just accepted a new church related to me the anger of some of his congregation when he introduced Scripture songs into their worship time. He hadn't replaced the music the people were familiar with but was only offering some new songs with biblical lyrics. On occasion, he asked the people to sing directly from their Bibles as he taught them lovely new melodies, thinking they would appreciate being able to carry God's Word in their hearts through song. Not so.

"We won't sing it if it isn't in the hymnal!" someone spouted. Their response was incredible!

Tragically, the congregation's clinging to tradition had so warped their viewpoint on worship that they didn't realize (1) they were being led by a faithful shepherd to do exactly what the Bible says and (2) however unwittingly, they were scorning God's own Word by their resistance. Peculiarly, they exalted a hymnal of brilliant but *human* inspiration above the eternal Word of *divine* inspiration.

I happen to know that particular pastor. Without question he was being sensitive when attempting to introduce new music with his congregation. However, many of us who have been through this process would have appreciated guidelines for teaching any new forms of worship. These have proved helpful:

1. *Give a biblical basis for what you introduce.* Show the idea in the Word itself, and show its practical benefits, too! People usually respond to truth when they see it, especially when seeing the potential promises within those things being taught.

2. *Don't try to accomplish too much, too fast.* The Bible likens people to sheep, not horses or cattle. Lead them slowly. Stampeding or rushing them creates unrest and will likely bring failure.

3. *Never propose something new as an opponent of something old.* When introducing new music, worship forms or songs, pushiness or arrogance about either the old or the new will never come across favorably. Lead into the

new from a positive base of love rather than from a
negative base of criticism of the old.

Singing Hymns

Our word "hymn" is derived from the Greek *humnois,* which is
simply the word for a religious song. Every generation writes its
own songs about the Lord and to Him; and whether in the first
or twenty-first century, hymns are songs of testimony, triumph,
exaltation, adoration and celebration.

Hymns were first defined to me as being (*a*) great doctrinal
statements set to music or (*b*) declarations of objective praise to
God. But I later learned a broader definition that was more
appropriate. Hymns span a wide range of music—wider than
some of us might like. For my part, I would prefer "Immortal,
Invisible, God Only Wise" to "I'll Fly Away, O Glory," and
"Blessed Assurance" to "Little Brown Church in the Vale."
Nonetheless, an honest definition derived from the New
Testament word requires latitude beyond individual tastes.

The distinct requirement of a Christian hymn is not its cal-
iber or quality but its subject matter. Technically, "hymn" refers
to the lyrics, while "melody," or "tune," refers to the song. But
whether sung or spoken, the subject is God—*His* grace, *His*
works, *His* purpose, *His* people, *His* power, *His* glory or *His* person. I don't recall being told this, but I apparently caught the
basic idea of hymns early in life, when I thought of them as
HIMs—songs about the Lord!

In some renewal congregations, the more classic, traditional
hymns have suffered disuse of late, hymnals often being discarded as irrelevant, musty artifacts of an unrenewed era. But as
surely as people become what they eat, a congregation becomes
what they sing; and there is something sturdy, durable and

THE CHURCH
NEEDS THE
STURDY,
ANCHOR-LIKE
HYMNS BORN
OF EARLIER
RENEWALS—
BUT TURTLE-
LIKE TEMPOS
SHOULD BE
SENT OUT TO
SEA FOREVER!

anchor-like about the hymns born of earlier renewals. We need them fused into our souls along with the newer songs in vogue today.

Older hymns sometimes "die" in church because of the way they're sung. A remedy? Don't drag them! There is nothing reverent about slow. Some people reject hymns simply because they are bored by them, but interest can be kept alive. Brisk and bright is better than dumpy and dead. I'm not appealing for jackrabbit jive or racehorse rhythms, but turtle-like tempos need to be sent out to sea forever!

Singing Spiritual Songs

There are wide differences in definition of "spiritual songs," and I don't want to appear either ignorant or critical of any of them. But I want to discuss my opinion that "spiritual songs" were the apostle Paul's reference to a distinct music form unique to the Church. It was one that would help fulfill the prospect of God's wanting to give everyone his or her own song of praise to Him.

Spiritual songs have been defined as informal choruses, choral anthems, simpler and more personal statements of faith or brief and noncomplex odes of worship. But I propose that they were—and are—a new music form unavailable until the New Testament, until Christ's full redemption allowed the Holy Spirit to dwell in mankind. Clearly, early believers sang "spiritual songs" of worship. But what were they?

Hodais pneumatikais, the exact phrase used in both Ephesians 5 and Colossians 3, is usually translated "spiritual songs." The first word is simply "ode," the Greek term for any words that were sung. But the second word, *pneumatikais*, seems to be the key to the full intended meaning of this phrase.

Pneumatikais—an obvious cognate to *pneuma* (spirit)—is most easily defined and understood by noting its use elsewhere in the New Testament. For example, Paul uses this word when introducing the subject of spiritual gifts in 1 Corinthians 12:1 (*pneumatika*, or "spiritual things"). Later, in his appeal to the Galatians concerning their duty to restore fallen brethren, the word *pneumatikoi* appears in the phrase "You who are spiritual" (Gal. 6:1). Although *pneumatika* occurs more than 20 times in the New Testament, these two texts give us something of a basic picture. *Pneumatika* seems to indicate Holy Spirit-filled people of character and charisma.

Their *character* is noted in the Galatian text:

Brethren, if a man is overtaken in any trespass, you who are spiritual restore such a one in a spirit of gentleness, considering yourself lest you also be tempted (Gal. 6:1).

Their *charisma* (in the sense of their functioning in the gifts of the Holy Spirit) is indicated in their apparent acceptance and response to spiritual things, i.e., manifestations of the Holy Spirit's gifts.

These factors alone would not finalize a definition, except for the fact that in this same context Paul discusses singing with the spirit. It is here in this classic passage, 1 Corinthians 12—14, as the apostle corrects the Corinthians' abuse of *glossolalia* ("native tongue"), that he also discusses singing of a distinctly Holy Spirit-enabled nature:

> For if I pray in a tongue, my spirit prays, but my understanding is unfruitful. What is the conclusion then? I will pray with the spirit, and I will also pray with the understanding. I will sing with the spirit, and I will also sing with the understanding (1 Cor. 14:14,15).

His distinguishing singing "with the spirit" from singing "with the understanding" points to what "spiritual songs" may have meant in the first-century Church: an exercise separate from, yet complementary to, the singing of psalms and hymns.

Because the general passage beginning in 1 Corinthians 12 and the specific text in 1 Corinthians 14 both use pneumatika to describe the kind of subject matter being dealt with, it follows that the distinct type of singing referred to as being "with the spirit" (pneuma) could be the same as "spiritual songs."

I would not be so bigoted as to oppose another interpretation, but I propose that the whole of the New Testament context supports the definition of "spiritual songs" as being Holy Spirit-enabled utterances that

were sung rather than spoken,

were a part of one's devotional life,

were explained or interpreted if exercised in corporate gatherings and

were so desirable as to have Paul assert his personal will to practice them: "I will sing with the spirit."

I would not preclude the possibility or desirability of spiritual songs being in the native language of the worshiper, nor would I suggest that one was preferable to another. But it does seem clear that the Holy Spirit is at work in this worship expression, doing something distinctly valid and valuable.

The practicality of this exercise is readily understandable when we remind ourselves how God has given the gift of worship for our edification as well as for His exaltation. It shouldn't surprise us that the gift of song for worship, praise, thanksgiving and adoration should provide at least one avenue for free, completely original, personal expression. Such spontaneity in personal worship may allow me the liberty of lyricizing my own heart's joy or pain, lifting it on a melody I spontaneously breathe forth. This kind of singing removes the restrictions of poetic rhyme, meter, rhythm and form. A practical, scriptural and desirable thing occurs: A previously unsung song—a new song—issues forth from worshiping lips, adoring Him and releasing the soul to broadened dimensions of glorifying the Creator.

Thus the spiritual song rounds out a triad of music forms given to the Church:

- In *psalms,* we declare His *Word* in song. We learn and rehearse the eternal, unchanging Word of His revealed truth in the Scriptures.
- In *hymns,* we announce His *works* in song. We praise Him and review His attributes, testifying to His goodness as experienced over the centuries.
- In *spiritual songs,* we welcome His *will* in song, giving place to the Holy Spirit's refilling and making place for His Word to dwell richly within.

Re-Choiring the Church

With such a variety of musical forms available to us, with music and song so universally enjoyed, with so unsurpassed an avenue for expressing human thought and emotion, why is music so often the focal point of problems or difficulty in the Church? Why is it so hard to get the people to learn new hymns, to sing joyously, to respond with spontaneity, to accept new musical forms? Why is the choir too loud or too soft, too difficult to understand, too ineffective or too overpowering? Why do we think the minister of music, the choral director or the organist "too demanding," "so undependable," "such a prima donna," "given to favoritism" and so on?

One approach that did more to expand our own horizons in corporate worship came about through repeated frustration and failure. Put simply, we couldn't get a choir to last.

Now, I love choral music very much. I enjoy hearing choirs and singing in them. Since my first experience leading a music group when I was six years old, I have helped form and lead choirs for everything from radio broadcasts to college tours, not to mention church. Yet, despite my best efforts, every early attempt to establish a choir at our pastorate in Van Nuys met with dismal results. We had no choir.

Each new try involved capable people. Each new beginning seemed exciting for everyone. But after three tries in as many years, I finally began to draw the conclusion that God was trying to tell me something.

So, I surrendered to the Lord the idea that we needed a choir. I don't suggest that what happened to us is the answer for every local church experiencing choral problems. But there is no question that God's declared moratorium on our efforts to form a choir became the key to unleashing the song of our congregation, for I asked the whole congregation to be our choir. I've already related how this tactic has allowed a freedom without foolishness, but that's how it all began.

I began to treat the church the way I would a choir. I started one Sunday by describing the conclusion I had reached following our repeated failures at choir formation. I didn't believe the vision for a congregation-wide choir was more spiritual than the usual approach. I didn't feel choirs were an unholy tradition that should be demolished, but rather that we were all to be the choir for that season in our body life. (Although we continue to treat the congregation as the choir, we now have two adult choirs—one traditional and one gospel—as well as children's choirs and youth ensembles.)

I did a couple of things to help our body apply this concept of the congregation as choir.

First, I taught from the Word of God. The book of Revelation unveils a massive angelic choir of worshipers in heaven: "And the number of them was ten thousand times ten thousand, and thousands of thousands" (Rev. 5:11). But the book of Hebrews goes further, amazingly putting us all among that heavenly choir, there at God's throne, sounding our praises beside the angelic voices and joining in the timeless worship of the Most High—*right now . . . every believer!*

> You have come to Mount Zion and to the city of the living God, the heavenly Jerusalem, to an innumerable company of angels (Heb. 12:22).

As these and other truths of the Word began to register, something came unshackled! Suddenly our congregation perceived themselves in a new light, joined to the heavenly choir of angels! Biblical truth had set them free to worship with a new sense of privilege and responsibility. I sometimes wonder if, more than we know, the presence of a good choir becomes an unintended substitute for a congregation's commitment to minister to the Lord. Our absence of a formed choir became a pivotal point to releasing everyone to be the choir.

Second, even today I often address the congregation as "choir." For example, I'll say, "Good morning! As we begin worship today, will the entire choir stand with me and. . . ." My gesture clearly encompasses the whole body and smiles come over their faces. Everyone knows what I mean, but if I see a bewildered visitor, I will add: "At The Church On The Way we've decided that the whole congregation will constitute the choir, so if you're visiting us today, join right in. We're not an exclusive group. In fact, some of us have terrible voices, but boy do we sing! Join in like you've been here a hundred years, and no one will know the difference."

This approach has done wonders toward solving one of any congregation's most challenging problems: how to get the people to learn new songs and hymns.

Most people are hesitant to attempt a new song. I guess we all have a residual fear of appearing foolish. Consequently, new songs are tough to introduce because the price of learning new music seems high. And it seems to take so long, going over and over a song. Thus, the flow and movement of the service suffers, especially if the song is ineptly taught or inappropriately introduced.

However, once the congregation perceives itself as the choir, a subtle but significant change occurs in the collective mind-set. To introduce a new hymn or worship chorus, I will say, "Choir, we're going to rehearse a new song. Don't worry about making mistakes—we're all learning it together. There's just one requirement: If you make a mistake, make a loud one." People laugh.

The atmosphere is relaxed, and with fear removed the learning process is speedy, fulfilling and, quite frankly, *fun*. Such a "re-choiring" of the body opens the way to spiritual advance. The corporate gathering is released into praise and worship, and each individual believer begins to view himself more seriously as a genuine minister to the Lord.

THE SHEER POWER OF SONG

There are places in the Bible where the sheer power of song explodes upon our understanding. I mean far more than the power of song to express joy, rejoicing, praiseful thanks or unified worship. I'm talking about song as an instrument of miracles—songs becoming works of power for *battle*, for *breakthrough* and for *birthing*.

The Song of Battle

The story of Judah's King Jehoshaphat and his victory over the invasion staged by the combined troops of Moab and Ammon is a great argument against the supposition that history is boring.

Vastly outnumbered by an alien host bent on their extermination, Jehoshaphat and his people made the Lord their first point of resort. With prayer and fasting they turned to Him, rather than appealing to a neighboring nation as a hired gun to come and rescue them. Their call to God was answered:

> Listen, all you of Judah and you inhabitants of Jerusalem, and you, King Jehoshaphat! Thus says the LORD to you: "Do not be afraid nor dismayed because of this great multitude, for the battle is not yours, but

God's. You will not need to fight in this battle. Position yourselves, stand still and see the salvation of the LORD, who is with you, O Judah and Jerusalem!" Do not fear or be dismayed; tomorrow go out against them, for the LORD is with you (2 Chron. 20:15,17).

Jehoshaphat and the people responded with awe and praise, but what makes this event memorable—and unique in the annals of military encounters—is the strategy they employed for battle.

The people of Judah took a peculiar action based in the raw conviction that God meant what He said: "You will not need to fight in this battle."

Jehoshaphat appointed a choir to go out before the army. *The singers preceded the warriors!*

The Lord did not dictate this arrangement; it's just that the people concluded this battle was different. Here's how it happened:

So they rose early in the morning . . . and as they went out, Jehoshaphat stood and said, "Hear me, O Judah and you inhabitants of Jerusalem: Believe in the LORD your God, and you shall be established; believe His prophets, and you shall prosper."

And when he had consulted with the people, he appointed those who should sing to the LORD, and who should praise the beauty of holiness, as they went out before the army and were saying: "Praise the LORD, for His mercy endures forever."

Now when they began to sing and to praise, the LORD set ambushes against the people of Ammon, Moab, and Mount Seir . . . and they were defeated. . . . They helped to destroy one another (2 Chron. 20:20-23).

God's people lifted their song of praise and expressed their belief in His promise. When they did, their enemies were so confounded by it all that they turned on one another!

It's a great story, but is it relevant to us today? Although some people are nervous about taking Old Testament events and applying the illustrated principles of faith to today's circumstances, I think there is truth here for us now. Let me elaborate.

Wynne Lewis is the former pastor of London's Kensington Temple, which is just down the road from Kensington Palace. He recently told me of a demanding season of spiritual struggle he and his congregation experienced some years ago.

An exceptional time of evangelism had brought burgeoning growth, attracting the attention of a band of spiritists in that part of London. An entire coven of witches began attempting an infiltration of the services at the Pentecostal church.

Anyone who knows the concentrated power of evil when demonic powers are focused against a holy enterprise can appreciate the invisible warfare that is ignited in such a setting. Wynne told me:

> One evening as I rose to preach, the oppression in the sanctuary was so strong I knew I must do something before beginning my message.
>
> The building was full, mostly with Christians committed to Christ's testimony. I said, "Brethren and sisters, I think you sense that we are facing a spiritual battle. You and I know that our strength is simply to lift up praise—to sing the overcoming song of our Lord Jesus' victory on the Cross."
>
> I began to lead the people, singing one song after another about the blood of Jesus, knowing that the Bible

teaches that hell is routed when believers exalt the blood of the Lamb at the heart of their testimony (see Rev. 12:11).

As we were singing, suddenly those who had been assigned to bind in an unholy agreement against God's free and powerful workings in that place began to rise and run from the room—hands over their ears against the praises of the saints. Needless to say, it was a night of great victory and salvation, and it brought a conclusion to that particular season of spiritual skirmish.

The song of the Lord is a mighty instrument for spiritual battle. The Lord would call us to worship Him with song when faced with an enemy that is too strong for us. We can see our worship become a musical power play and find victory in our circumstances as we obey the directive to worship with song. It's a timeless resource which God's Word reveals as a powerful part of the arsenal He has given for our triumph in spiritual conflict.

The Song of Breakthrough

The breakthrough of the gospel into Europe in the first century was supernatural by every criteria.

It began as the result of a Holy Spirit-inspired vision that led Paul and his party to move west instead of east in their evangelistic pursuits.

It was birthed at the edge of a river as God's Word was preached and confirmed by His power and His followers gained their first European converts.

Their efforts were assailed by a repeated and deceptive testimony shouted from the lips of a demon-possessed woman, whose sorceries had gained influence over many in that area. But the sorceress was delivered from satanic torments when Paul cast the demon from her, setting the woman free to follow Christ.

For their act of mercy, manifest in that act of exorcism, Paul and Silas were cast into prison, a clear effort of the recently expelled demon to restrain further gospel advance into its principality—the doorway to an entire continent.

From within their prison cell, the two beaten and bound missionaries began to sing praises to God. As they sang, an earthquake shook the area, resulting in the miracle of their jailer's repentance and the conversion of his entire household (see Acts 16:16-34).

This cluster of events burst forth like pressed grapes, letting flow the wine of Holy Spirit operations of power that established a beachhead for the gospel on a new continent. Though it seems impossible to cite any single event as pivotal in the spread of Christianity, one idea shines through clearly: The original breakthrough of the gospel westward into Europe was not achieved without an apostolic experience in the sheer power of song.

Not every analyst may relate the singing of Paul and Silas to their miraculous deliverance from the jail. However, note how the Bible

SONG IS A MIGHTY MEANS OF BREAK-THROUGH AND LIBERATION.

supports the proposition that such may have been the case; song is a mighty means of breakthrough and liberation:

> You are my hiding place; You shall preserve me from trouble; You shall surround me with songs of deliverance (Ps. 32:7).

> The LORD is my strength and song, and He has become my salvation (Exod. 15:2).

> "Behold, God is my salvation, I will trust and not be afraid, for YAH, the LORD, is my strength and song; He also has become my salvation." Therefore with joy you will draw water from the wells of salvation (Isa. 12:2,3).

A close examination of these and other passages shows that songs are not only offerings of praise for what God has done, but these are also instruments of our present partnering with His almightiness *unto deliverance*. In Psalm 32:7 we are told that the Lord hides us and preserves us from trouble by encircling us with songs of deliverance. Somehow in ways which defy our analysis, the song of the Lord on the lips of His people has a potential for contributing to spiritual overthrow, upheaval and breakthrough. Just as music in the physical realm may strike a wavelength that shatters glass, so songful worship in the spiritual realm can shake Satan's dominion, toppling principalities of hell and extending the kingdom of God through Jesus Christ!

The Song of Birthing

Isaiah 54 opens with a paradoxical command—"Sing, O barren, you who have not borne!"—the irony being that no one would direct a despairing reject to sing.

In ancient Israel, nothing prompted song less than the barren condition of a woman. A woman without children was disenfranchised, discredited, suspect of spiritual unworthiness and potentially subject to divorce—all on the grounds of her biological incapability for childbearing. Into this depressing situation of personal hopelessness, the prophet commands the woman to sing and, incredibly, directs her to start preparing a nursery for there are babies (plural) coming!

> Enlarge the place of your tent. . . . For you shall expand to the right and to the left, and your descendants will inherit the nations. . . . You will forget the shame of your youth. . . . For your Maker is your husband, the LORD of hosts is His name (Isa. 54:2-5).

An entire spool of thought unrolls a continuous thread of blessing, which is promised to follow upon the heels of song alone! A tapestry of joy including multiple births is prophesied, complete with promises of widespread fruit and joyous consequences flowing from the midst of the singer's song.

This passage of promise is far more than poetry.

Here is the declaration of a principle that shines from other passages in the Word of God, for song and birth—praises and new life—are linked together time and again. The cause-and-effect relationship is not always the same; but God being the author of all that is, the issue raised is not our *sequence* in song but the *suffocation* of song. The Bible reveals that songlessness—depression, defeat, discouragement, despair—restricts the possible inflow of new life. The spirit of heaviness blankets souls and suffocates hope. But song has a power to explode despair and expand a space for hope to begin.

From the "birth" of creation, when God's creative activity was accompanied by music, as "the morning stars sang together, and all the sons of God shouted for joy" (Job 38:7), to the birth-time songs of Hannah and Mary (see 1 Sam. 2:1-10; Luke 1:46-55), song and new life are joined together. The distinctive thing about Isaiah's words is that the song he calls for is not just a joyous response to an impending birth; the song declares the promise and sets the atmosphere for its fulfillment! There is a possibility in song's sheer dynamic that continues to this day.

WHEN THE BARREN SANG

It doubtless seemed like just another Sunday as Mike and Cheri were seated with the congregation that day over a decade ago. I didn't know them at all—they were new to our assembly, and it would be a full year until I actually met them.

They probably weren't thinking about the matter that morning, but the fact was that Mike and Cheri were unable to have children. Medical examination had indicated that it was very unlikely they would ever enjoy the parental privilege short of adopting a baby.

Of course, I knew nothing of these facts, nor of their prayerful desire that after 11 years of marriage they might conceive a child.

That day my subject was "The Conceiving and Bearing of Life." It wasn't really a message on having children but on overcoming any barrenness in the bleak spots of our lives. Isaiah 54 was my text, and I discussed God's call to worship and to praise Him at any point of our lives that seems hopelessly unfruitful. During my delivery of the message, something very special took place.

My understanding of at least one manifestation of the spiritual gift called "a word of knowledge" (1 Cor. 12:8) is that the Holy Spirit will give someone *both* supernatural insight *and* a corresponding promise from God regarding the issue being revealed. That's exactly what happened while I was preaching.

I paused midway through the sermon, sensing the Holy Spirit's presence and prompting. Then I spoke. "Church," I said, "I need to interrupt myself for just a moment.

"My message has specifically *not* had to do with natural childbearing but with life flowing into barren parts of our lives in other respects. Still, the Holy Spirit is impressing upon me that there is a couple here this morning who has longed for a child, who has been told they cannot have one and whom the Lord wants to know He is present to speak to your need in a personal way this morning. His word to you is this: 'Begin to fill your house with song, and as you do, the life-giving power of that song will establish a new atmosphere and make way for the conception which you have desired.'"

I didn't ask anyone to indicate his or her personal situation or response to that word. Rather, I simply went on with the message as I had planned, basically forgetting about the incident until nearly a year later.

I engaged Mike and Cheri in conversation a few days prior to the Sunday they were to present their baby girl for dedication. I had never had a conversation with them, and it was especially nice to talk with them because they were so excited about their baby. After brief opening exchanges, Mike came to the point.

"Pastor Jack, we wanted to talk with you for a few minutes because of this Sunday's dedication of our baby. There's something about it we felt you would want to know." With that, he recounted the episode of that Sunday about 11 months before— of their childlessness, their prayer, the Holy Spirit's word to them and their baby.

"Pastor," Mike continued, "we went home that day and began to do what the Holy Spirit instructed us. We began to fill our house with song. Cheri and I would walk hand in hand into each room and simply sing praises and worship to the Lord. We just wanted you to know that the baby we're bringing for presentation to the Lord this Sunday is the fruit of that song, that the Lord did fulfill His word given that morning."

Can you imagine how I rejoiced with them?

How gracious our Lord and how tender His ways!

That baby's birth was a holy phenomenon not conjured up by man's efforts or enthusiasm. But it was the precious fruit of one couple's natural union that, until the divinely appointed song of the Lord entered their situation, had not found the fruitfulness for which they longed.

And so we dedicated the baby. But there's one last footnote to the story.

It's about Aimee. Remember the little eight-year-old girl who came to the prayer room door and signaled that she wanted to talk with me and who then sang me the song the Lord had given to her?

I was especially touched that morning as little Aimee went back out the door, for as her song was echoing in my ears, I was praising God for the life-begetting power of song. I was reveling in how it can transmit from one generation to another where simple childlike hearts—and congregations—will welcome it.

For, you see, Aimee is Mike and Cheri's daughter. She is the baby who was born as a result of their filling the house with song, even after years of barrenness without hope.

She was the fruit of a song—a song that now was finding a place in her young life.

Who knows what richness her song will bring in the years that follow?

Who knows what a new song may bring to you?

CHAPTER 12

BEYOND ALL WORLDS... HERE AND NOW

Above and beyond all the realm of time and space, Above earthly limits, beyond this world's embrace, A life may be found which with power will abound, If you believe, you can receive power to live above and beyond.

To say that he had been born with a silver spoon in his mouth would have exaggerated the point, but there is no doubt that Solomon had an edge over most of his contemporaries. As the beloved Bathsheba's son, he was the living reminder of God's forgiveness and grace toward his father, King David. Though he was the second child of a marriage spawned in adultery and murder, the guilt of the past had been flushed away with the tragic death of his brother—the firstborn to this union which was tarnished in its inception and scarred from its establishment.

But now David was dead.

In a flurry of political jockeying, including the diplomatic intervention of Zadok the priest and Nathan the prophet, the crown was conferred upon Solomon and the self-seeking takeover attempt of his half-brother Adonijah was averted.

With a humility characteristic of his father, the fledgling ruler sought God's wisdom rather than wealth, and the early stages of his leadership were marked with divine blessing.

Solomon finished the Temple.

No greater monument could be built in testimony to the combined devotion of both David and Solomon. The temporary Tabernacle David had established was but a forecast of his highest desire—the building of a permanent dwelling place for the manifest presence of the Lord God of Israel. That for which David's planning and financial provision had paved the way, Solomon pursued to completion with equal commitment. And the day the Temple was dedicated, God's pleasure with it all was abundantly evidenced:

> King Solomon, and all the congregation . . . [were] sacrificing sheep and oxen that could not be counted or numbered for multitude. Then the priests brought in the ark of the covenant of the LORD. . . . And it came to pass, when the priests came out of the holy place, that the cloud filled the house of the LORD, so that the priests could not continue ministering because of the cloud; for the glory of the LORD filled the house of the LORD (1 Kings 8:5,6,10,11).

There is no question of God's pleasure with the worship, the worshipers and the house of worship. The visitation of the Lord and the manifestation of His glory in response to this occasion fully verify the propriety of it all. Not only is Solomon's desire to honor God confirmed by the Almighty's presence and display, but also the same event ought to permanently silence any proposition that large expenditures for church buildings may displease God. David and Solomon's whole project translates to a cost of approximately $4 trillion![1]

THE WORTHINESS OF WORSHIP

A special poignancy surrounds that dedication day, especially in the awe-inspired words of Solomon's dedicatory prayer (see 1 Kings 8:22-54). Kneeling and with his hands spread upward in worship, he brings an impassioned appeal that calls for God's presence, blessing and mercy to reside among his people. Midway through the prayer, Solomon makes a simple statement which breaks the back of any skeptic's notion that Israel saw Yahweh merely as a tribal deity. Having invited the Lord's abiding presence into the Temple, he says:

> But will God indeed dwell on the earth? Behold, heaven and the heaven of heavens cannot contain You. How much less this temple which I have built! (v. 27).

It's here I invite you to pause with me—here at the dedication of Solomon's Temple. To pause meditatively where those words were first spoken is to be wisely taught, for the worthiness of worship is demonstrated here as in few other places. The event yields a fourfold statement on worth in worship.

1. A *material* declaration of worth is made in the enormous investment the structure represents, all of it being the direct result of offerings brought by devoted worshipers of the Lord.

2. A *spiritual* declaration of worth is seen in the overwhelming number of sacrifices offered that day as they sanctified this new house unto God.

3. A *conceptual* grasp of God's worth is evidenced in Solomon's statement on the grandeur of God's person and nature, as his dedicatory prayer acknowledges His omnipotence and transcendence and rests its faith in the attributes of God's love, mercy and faithfulness.

4. A *dynamic* demonstration of God's declaration of worth shines forth in His visitation of glory, the seal of His presence and the affirmation of His acceptance of this worship as truly worthy.

KEEPING WORSHIP WORTHY

There is a two-edged problem in seeking to ensure our worship is sufficiently worthy.

On the one hand, there is a contemporary tendency toward the inappropriately casual, which may claim to be simple but actually becomes trite, glib and occasionally cutesy at times of praise and worship. The most sincere leader can contribute to the evolution of a less-than-worthy view of God among those he leads unless cautioned against the possibility of people's misreading his casual style. The desire to sustain a bright, positive atmosphere can too easily destroy occasions for deep heart searching and holy contemplation of God's greatness and holiness. An upbeat spirit and mood is appropriate, assuming it doesn't beget a deadbeat slovenliness of mind toward God's person and glorious attributes. But since a predisposition toward the informal can unwittingly cultivate an insensitivity toward the One to whom worshipers come, I want to lead toward and to participate in worship which commands our entire thought, our most sensitive devotion and our reverential fear.

On the other hand, some react strongly to perceived shallowness allowed in certain settings. I must be careful to guard against criticizing those without the "theological enlightenment" I may feel is important to worthy worship, lest such a reaction produce a self-righteous quest for excellence that can easily dissolve into an equal, though opposite, carnality.

Pride is not superior to shallowness, and perceived superficiality cannot effectively be countered by labored efforts at being "deep." Depth is not the product of brainpower or social style but only results from a genuine desire for God's honor and not a vindication of viewpoint. However great my devotion to "redignifying" worship, God will never be impressed by my worthy efforts if they smack of a secret sense of superiority above the worship style of any other of His children.

WEORTHSCIPE

Weorthscipe. That Old English word meant "to ascribe worth, to pay homage, to reverence or to venerate." It inevitably turns up in any search for the real meaning of worship, for it addresses the issue of worth—of ascribed worthiness in worship—and it asks questions of us who worship:

1. What value are you placing here? Is the manner of honoring the One being worshiped proportionate to His character and attributes?

2. Do our praises as worshipers indicate an awareness of the traits inherent in the One we extol? What is present of adoration—of plain, heartfelt, emotional love and affection?

3. Does our worship involve genuine devotion or is it only intellectualized—in truth but not in Spirit? The *fuel* of our worship may be our understanding, but the *fires* of worship are ignited from the heart and not the mind.

How shall we bring worthy worship to the Most Worthy One? Solomon's Temple is a good place to come to learn of weorthscipe. It is the scene where three great themes of worship are shown, all of which emphasize God's worthiness and necessitate a reformation in the way we worship. Consider the *transcendence*, the *transaction* and the *transformation* involved in worthy worship.

The Transcendence of God

God's transcendence describes His beyondness: Though He is present everywhere He is also beyond all worlds. He who created all things is separate from and existent beyond His creation. When we say God is present *in* the midst of His creation, it is not the same as saying He is present *within* it. The former makes Him our present help, the truly personal being He is, who desires to dwell among His own and to manifest His love and power in their interest. The latter depersonalizes Him, claiming to contain Him within His own handiwork, as though God was literally in the fragrance of flowers, the tenderness of a baby or the grandeur of the starry heavens.

Anyone who supposes God to be a part of His own creation is in error, but it is also erroneous to suppose it an exaltation of

His greatness to forget or neglect the truth of His immediacy, because He is in fact personally interested in, cares for and is with each of us.

It is well and wise that in our worship we take time to know and enjoy the wonder of God's personal attributes. Entire books are written on the different aspects of His nature, the qualities of His character and the attributes of His being, for there is no way the marvel of God's greatness can be exhausted by human analysis. Still, theological expertise isn't a prerequisite to worship God, but a hunger to know Him *is*. Intellectualizing God's traits does not certify a more worthy worship, but passive indifference or mere excitement will miss the mark, too. We are called to neither a mind trip nor an emotional binge. Let Holy Spirit-filled worship be a blend of our highest thoughts and our deepest feelings so that one of the goals of true worship be reached: *the reshaping of our lives.*

Because human nature inevitably becomes like the object of its worship, an ever-deepening perspective on our Father's nature enhances the likelihood of those qualities being formed in us. Thoughtful comment by sensitive worship leaders can stimulate such growth, expanding the praise and increasing the insight of those who join them in worship. Well-stated, concise remarks in introducing a chorus or hymn help in this regard.

Anna is unusually gifted at this.

Through the years of our ministry, it hasn't been uncommon on a Sunday morning, as my wife leads our people in the selected hymn-of-the-day, for her to pause between two verses and make a personal observation or relate a pithy anecdote. The effect is often dramatic, and the next verse ignites as an aspect of God's goodness is refreshed in our thoughts. The secret to her effectiveness is her simplicity and brevity. She knows this is no time for a homily, but her sensitivity overflows and awakens that same sense in the whole congregation.

Let us learn to meditate on God's power, His love, His wisdom, His holiness, His changelessness, His mercy, His glory. You might have the opportunity to invite other worshipers to do so with you. "Let's pause before we sing this again, and let the Holy Spirit help you recall some way in which God's *almightiness* has met you at specific points." (The same could be done with any trait appropriate to the hymn, chorus or song being sung.) His personal traits will be most quickly perceived when related to the worshiper's experience rather than related only as theological concepts. Living worship can be set aflame when sparked by expanding perspectives on our Father's attributes.

An increased deepening of praise, worship and thanksgiving is inevitable where worshipers are led to think on the manifold splendor of the Eternal One, our God. Let us kneel to worship . . . let us rise to praise Him—

> the Almighty and Self-Sufficient One,
> the Entirely Holy Three-In-One,
> the Merciful, the Righteous and the Just,
> the All-Knowing and All-Wise,
> the Essence and Fountain of Love,
> the Creator and Lord of Hosts,
> the Absolute and Changeless One,
> the Transcendent and the Immanent One,
> the True and Faithful One—

who, in all His wonder, grandeur and excellence,

> has chosen to love us,
> has sought to redeem us and
> has sent His Son to us:

JESUS CHRIST
THE ONE AND ONLY SAVIOR

He has become our Father through the new birth He has made
possible in Christ,

> who was born of the virgin,
> lived sinlessly,
> taught truthfully and
> died vicariously for mankind;
> whose blood and death are the ransom price paid for me,
> providing completely for my eternal salvation.

He is the Son of God,

> who literally and physically rose from the dead,
> who has ascended to the right hand of the Majesty on high and
> who has poured out His Holy Spirit of power upon us,
> that we might live in grace both now and forever.
> Let the Father be praised!
> Let His Son be worshiped!
> Let His Spirit be manifest among us!

Our Transactions with God

Worthy worship begins with a focus on the greatness of God and
His goodnesses to us. But there is a critical juncture at which
worship requires a transaction—a very real piece of business
must take place.

Sacrifice. Offering. There is no such thing as worship without there being something very tangible brought from man's
side.

Worship may be fulfilling, enriching, soul stirring, enlight-
ening, healing, refreshing, restful, invigorating or any of the
innumerable other beneficial results that heartfelt worship real-
izes. But because God doesn't require payment for His blessings
and because His gifts cannot be bought, worship can become a

joy to our souls, a healing to our hearts and a balm to our minds; and yet we still have not made any definitive investment ourselves. As filled with blessing and beauty as such worship may be for a season, if worshipers are not brought to an understanding of their responsibility in giving, the loveliest worship will eventually evaporate into thin air and thin souls.

Solomon's Temple reminds us that worthy worship involves a material investment. It is significant that this glorious structure, so overflowingly filled with God's far more glorious presence, was built on the site of a business transaction made by his father David—a transaction made in the interest of worship. The Temple was constructed on land which had already become a place of a redemptive sacrifice in worship and of a willing sacrifice of wealth. David said to Araunah as he sought to secure the property for the purpose of sacrifice to God, "I will not offer to the Lord my God that which costs me nothing" (see 2 Sam. 24:24). Araunah's offer to freely give his king the land was graciously rejected by David. He knew worship should have a worthiness that includes an open hand as well as an open heart.

We cannot escape the need to repeatedly affirm the principle of tangible, material giving being properly associated with worship under the New Covenant. Human nature instinctively fears giving. This is not so much stinginess as self-protection, and our worship of God is a means for our deliverance from that fear—if we'll accept it. The cost is our honest confrontation with any residual fear of giving. The tender teaching of the truth, spoken in the spirit of God's love for us all, can set people free to give in worship and to live in worshipful givingness.

The offering of an animal under the Old Testament order was symbolic of Christ's then-future sacrifice for our sin. The grace it promised was not being bought thereby but being anticipated. Because of this we often overlook a very basic fact: For all intents and purposes, the ancient sacrifice was a "cash" transaction. In an agricultural society, nothing represented a more specific expenditure of personal property than an animal from your herd. As obvious as this is, hosts of New Testament believers today live out a relatively unsacrificial lifestyle in terms of their worship transactions.

At times there seems to be undue diligence in the attempt to demolish biblical disciplines about money. No subject has been more debated or subjected to self-styled privileges of personal deviation in practice than church giving—offerings, tithes, special funds, etc. A basic tendency is as persistent today as it was in Cain and Abel's day—while some give obediently, others still insist on their own opinions and demand that God receive their offerings on their own terms. Appealing to our no longer being under the Law regarding financial sacrifice seems to violate the concept of grace.

Peculiarly, some contend on the grounds of the New Testament for the abolition of the discipline of the tithe. Tithing is assailed as though its teaching were a dangerous legalism rather than a liberating truth. I've seen worshipers, who are enjoying a reformation in freed and freeing song and praise, suddenly wince when tithes and offerings are received, as though it were a materialistic degradation of their "pure worship"—an imposition of legalistic demands on otherwise liberated believers. That's not a reformation; it's a rebellion!

Truly reformed, biblical worship is not secured in our souls until it cuts across our fear and our selfishness. Planned, persistent, disciplined, faithful, obedient giving is the sword that can cut away superficiality, loose us from doubt and disobedience and cause the spirit of sacrifice to fuel a revival in our lives.

Tithes and offerings are as incumbent upon the New Testament believer as upon worshipers in earlier eras. Why?

- Jesus Himself confirmed the practice of tithing as being valid, joining to it the high promise of God's abundance being poured back upon His disciples who would learn the release that comes through worshipful giving (see Matt. 23:23; Luke 6:38).
- New Testament believers are called to walk in the steps of Abraham, the first Bible character to practice tithing as a response to God's blessing upon his life (see Gen. 14:18-22; Rom. 4:12; Heb. 7:4-6).
- Systematic and proportional giving were taught in the Gentile church as disciplines that released the ministry of the Church to serve human need. This was done willingly even though almost all Old Testament ordinances were unrequired of them (see Acts 15:22-29; 1 Cor. 16:2).
- The glory of the New Covenant at no point retreats from the character values of the Old but enhances and expands them. In terms of giving, we would logically expect an increase or, at the very least, no retreat or reduction of disciplined giving patterns (see 2 Cor. 3:9,11).
- There are promised blessings related to the giving of tithes and offerings. And they are not less applicable when they are found in the Old Testament (see Mal. 3:8-12; 2 Cor. 1:20).

The transaction of tithes and offerings is no small issue. Where people are being reformed in worship, giving is and will be dramatically released. If it isn't, the worship reformation may not be suspect, but it will be short-lived. Tithing and giving may not guarantee the presence of a spirit of worship, but their absence can guarantee its eventual withering.

But there's even more to this matter of worship's transaction.

* * * * *

Today's reform is fostering a return in the Church to biblical freedom in the physical expressions of worship.

Just the other day I had the privilege of watching one of the executives in our congregation present a seminar for other business leaders. This man represents one of today's best-known corporations and travels internationally to help them solve their problems. As he began the seminar, he looked out at these cool-headed, calculating executives and said, "I'm going to ask for your response, and I'm going to want you to put some meat on the table." What he meant was that he wanted them to *act* in response to his questions and invitations to interaction—to actuate and activate their thoughts with physical acknowledgment. This is the essence of God's call to "present your bodies." He clearly wants us to demonstrate our understanding with responses that involve our hands as well as our hearts and our heads—our bodies as well as our beliefs.

The Bible is very explicit that we are to involve ourselves physically in worship—another confrontation with our fears. In Psalm 50:5 the Lord says, "Gather My saints together to Me, those who have made a covenant with Me by sacrifice." In the Old Testament, worshipers offered sacrifices of animals and grain, but that was not all that was required; the worshiper also came with praise and thanksgiving (see Ps. 107:22).

In Philippians 2:17, Paul speaks of himself as being a sacrifice. Of course, when he wrote to the Philippians, Paul was in prison and knew that imminent death was a very real possibility. Martyrdom is perhaps the most dramatic example of sacrifice and, yes, there are believers in the world today who live under oppressive regimes, knowing that they may be called at any time to make a literal sacrifice of their lives for their faith. But no matter where we live, each of us is directed to no less than complete sacrifice of ourselves to the Lord:

> I beseech you therefore, brethren, by the mercies of God, that you present your *bodies* a living *sacrifice*, holy, acceptable to God, which is your reasonable service (Rom. 12:1, emphasis mine).

PHYSICAL EXPRESSIONS OF PRAISE ONCE WRITTEN OFF AS "CALISTHENICS" ARE NOW BECOMING ACCEPTED AS TIMELESS AND VALID FOR THE WHOLE CHURCH.

Physical expressions of praise that have traditionally been absent from our worship services, or categorically written off as "calisthenics," are now becoming accepted as timeless and valid for the whole Church. Many of us are learning to include another transaction in our worship—the offering of our bodies as a living sacrifice, humbly presented in worship.

Kneeling was once avoided by evangelical Protestants as being too "high church," reserved only for a penitent at the altar following an invitation. Now its practice is filling our worship services and prayer meetings. Such songs as "Come Let Us Worship and Bow Down," "I Will Come and Bow Down" and "No Higher Calling" point the way and encourage us to do what we are singing.

Upraised hands, once resisted by most of the Church and consigned to oblivion by all but Pentecostals and charismatics, are realizing a beautiful and orderly use everywhere. People are responding to the apostle Paul's wish: "I would that all men everywhere lift up holy hands" (1 Tim. 2:8).

Applause and rhythmic handclapping, the most natural physical expression of human joyfulness, are being allowed in an increasing circle of the faithful. Once deemed irreverent or superficial, the reformation is not only applying the biblical commandment to offer such praises, but it is also allowing the possibility that such humanness as "clapping for joy" is a God-created tendency put within man and, therefore, appropriate for praising Him.

These physical expressions are part of the transaction of worship because they actually involve an investment—the spending of more of our whole selves, presenting our bodies, often at the expense of our pride. A holy liberation is unleashing a full-spectrum worship, expressed by the awakening of the *whole human being*—spirit, soul, mind *and* body.

Our Transformation Before God

God gave the glorious manifestation of His presence at the dedication of Solomon's Temple as more than merely a resplendent, awe-inspiring sight. The Scriptures reveal God's glory as meant *for* us—to touch us, to affect and to transform us.

The ultimate purpose in God's glory shown toward man is defined in Jesus Christ. He is God's conclusive display of glory, and with His coming the qualities and purpose of that glory are described:

> And the Word became flesh and dwelt [literally, "taber-nacled"] among us, and we beheld His glory, the glory of the only begotten of the Father, full of grace and truth (John 1:14).

His glory, filled with grace and truth, makes God's glory not only our object in worship but also our source of blessing. His glory is given to overflow us with grace and truth—grace which meets us where we are and truth that sets us free to become! His glory is given to transform us, not entertain us. Where bruise, bondage or affliction are present, worship welcomes the glory of God—His excellence of power to redeem, restore and reinstate:

> Where the Spirit of the Lord is, there is liberty. But we all, with unveiled face, beholding as in a mirror the glory of the Lord, are being transformed into the same image from glory to glory, just as by the Spirit of the Lord (2 Cor. 3:17,18).

He who transcends all worlds comes to transform us. He is here to liberate—to scatter our fears, overthrow our doubt, strengthen our weakness and explode sin and self-imposed restrictions.

Our worship is His means to lift us out of ourselves. Not to some euphoric mysticism, cultish meditation, demonic astral travel or humanistic quest for supra-consciousness, but to come before His throne and permit the glory of His power to progressively change our hearts, our attitudes, our thought patterns and our character deficiencies.

He means to transform us, turning
our fears into our resting in His love,
our pride into our waiting at His feet,
our weakness into our discovery of His grace,
our pain into a healing of our whole personalities,
our doubt into a new faith in His faithfulness.

That's what worship's transformation is: God's way to transmit wholeness, in which we come to realize the meaning of worshiping "in the beauty of holiness" (Ps. 29:2).

HOLY, HOLY, HOLY

It was a century and a half after Solomon stood within the courts of the newly finished Temple that another young man was at worship in the same building. Suddenly, captivated by the spirit of worship, Isaiah saw a vision of the Lord:

I saw the Lord sitting on a throne, high and lifted up,
and the train of His robe filled the temple (Isa. 6:1).

Isaiah continues by describing the angelic beings worshiping around the Creator's throne, who ceaselessly lift their voices in continuous praise: "Holy, holy, holy is the LORD of hosts; the whole earth is full of His glory!" (v. 3).

Isaiah relates his suddenly being stricken with a sense of his unworthiness as the pure power of God's presence shakes the place.

Woe is me, for I am undone! Because I am a man of unclean lips, and I dwell in the midst of a people of unclean lips; for my eyes have seen the King, the LORD of hosts (v. 5).

As Isaiah looks upon the holiness of the Almighty, His awe in worship suddenly turns to shame for sin. He becomes deeply aware of all the things he isn't, as he looks upon all the things God is. What follows is as heart-touching a scene as any in the Bible, for it provides a lovely study in the transforming power of worship. The response of the Most Holy God to that worshiper's confession is as mighty in meaning as it is merciful in manner.

Isaiah has confessed the impurity of his lips, and the words of despair have hardly been spoken when instantly—without a word of condemnation or a moment of hesitation—the living God responds. An angel is commissioned to take a coal from heaven's altar and apply its purifying flame to the point of Isaiah's confessed need and concern.

Truth flashes here like lightning!

The prophet's experience teaches us for all time that our failures are not barricades to our approaching the Holy One. Worship allows the unworthy to come before God in the full expectation that His holy wholeness will answer to our unwhole unholiness. Just as with Isaiah, living worship will increase our sense of His holiness and our unworthiness, but it also makes room for a transforming encounter which will purge our sin. Isaiah found the fire of God applied to the specific point of his need, and we can expect the same. He will halt the flow of sinning from any part of our lives.

With Isaiah it was his lips. Where do you need purifying?

At the cross we find saving forgiveness through Christ's blood, but at the altar of worship we can find sanctifying holiness through the Holy Spirit's fire. Encounters like Isaiah's receive the assurance of God's love, forgiveness for sin and direction for the future. In such transforming worship God reveals the way His transcendent, glorious holiness has come to penetrate our world—all of it.

Hear it! See it! Isaiah invites us all to share his encounter with God's glory.

Listen, loved one!

Glory is what we all lost when we lost touch with God.

Glory is what we all seek—the recovery of that loss.

But our fumbling, bumbling ways of going about regaining the glory is a study in human frustration and in human sinning. Man seeks glory down labyrinthine ways of selfish, willful, prideful and blind pursuits. The quest for what we might become is so often pursued outside the presence of the very One who holds the key to our becoming.

But now He invites us to glory.

The heavenly call to worship is not the demanding directive of a deity concerned for His own glory. His call to come into His glorious presence is born of His concern over *our* glory; He desires that our loss of glory may be restored by our welcoming His. God is ready to pour His glory upon us, purge us with its fire, overflow us with its power and bring us to His created purpose for our lives!

That's why He keeps saying, "Remember."

CHAPTER 13

REMEMBERING WHAT TO REMEMBER

Until He comes again, His death will I proclaim. I will eat this bread and I
will drink this wine Until He comes again . . . until He comes again.

We were late for church.

As we rather apologetically slipped into a row near the back, our five-year-old son, Mark, slid onto the seat next to mine. Anna and I were both somewhat bleary-eyed. The whole family had just been ravaged by a post-Christmas siege of flu, and we had thought at first we would stay home that morning. Either guilt or grace, I don't know which, got us going in time to at least make the last service.

It was New Year's Sunday. And I didn't know a miracle was about to happen.

Communion is always served at our church on the first Sunday of the month. We call it that—Communion, or the Lord's Table. For others it's called Eucharist or the Mass, and it is observed at widely differing intervals and in very different ways, depending upon which group you worship with. As it turned out, this time for us was to be very memorable.

At that time, I was teaching at LIFE Bible College in Los Angeles and had no pastoral duties on Sunday. Our tardy family was seated near the rear in the spacious auditorium of Angelus Temple when Communion began to be served. As the pastor read from Scripture, I listened again to the apostle Paul's instruction:

> For I received from the Lord that which I also delivered to you: that the Lord Jesus on the same night in which He was betrayed took bread; and when He had given thanks, He broke it and said, "Take, eat; this is My body which is broken for you; do this in *remembrance of Me.*"
>
> In the same manner He also took the cup after supper, saying, "This cup is the new covenant in My blood. This do, as often as you drink it, in *remembrance of Me.*"
>
> For as often as you eat this bread and drink this cup, you proclaim the Lord's death till He comes (1 Cor. 11:23-26, emphasis mine).

The reading of the passage refreshed my memory of the fact that Paul had called this event a proclamation, a declaration— literally a preaching of Christ until He returns again. The Greek verb Paul uses, *katangello*, means to preach or proclaim and is dramatic in its etymology, as the second part of the verb is the same word as "angel." Somehow that dramatizes the message-bearing potential implicit in the action of Communion. Paul taught that Communion is a proclamation, a sermon, a preachment—a message of life centered in a commemoration of a death. The morning worship continued.

Prayer was offered, and as the congregation was led to concertedly praise God for the provisions of the Cross, a spirit of expectancy filled the room. While ushers began distributing the bread and the cup, we sang a chorus of exaltation to Jesus Himself.

There were more people there than on an average Lord's Day—there always were on Communion Sunday. Our people seemed to appreciate the life and joy this feature of worship always held when we celebrated the Lord's Table.

My mind turned to my son seated beside me, at age five appearing rather oblivious to the proceedings of the made-for-adults service in progress. We were so late that we had opted against dropping him off in children's church. We were shortly to discover the gracious providence in that decision.

"Son," I said, anticipating the arrival of the bread tray which was now being passed down the row just ahead of us, "do you know what we're all doing right now?" He looked at me rather blankly, his expression indicating that he really didn't notice that *anything* was happening now.

I continued. "We're having Communion today and Daddy's gonna help you, so you can take Communion with the rest of the people."

He brightened, looking expectant. "Good," I smiled, actually wondering how much of Mark's response might be his knowing he was going to get to drink from "one of those little glasses." Then somehow I began to sense this was meant to be an unusual moment and I wondered if I shouldn't take time—then and there—to help him understand about those little bits of crackers and tiny cups.

I took two pieces of the bread in my hand, and as the tray came with the cups, I nodded to the usher. "I'm explaining Communion to my son," I whispered. "I'll return the cups after the service."

The elderly man recognized me, smiled graciously and moved on without interrupting what turned out to be a miracle moment in our family's life.

Communion is always special. And New Year's Sunday always has a "brand-newness" written all over it. But before this New Year's Communion day was over, I would be walking home beside my son—both of us having shared a distinctly joyous experience.

Mark received Jesus Christ as his Savior that morning!

Of course, Mark wouldn't say—now *or* then—that he was born again through taking Communion. Anyone understanding God's Word knows that participating in a Christian ordinance doesn't gain salvation. But the Lord's Table does preach it, and Mark heard the message loud and clear that day. It happened as people worshiped in an atmosphere of faith, fullness and joy and as I took time to explain the message in the elements:

"Mark, this bread is to remind us of Jesus' body. This cup of grape juice is to remind us of Jesus' blood." I spoke slowly, watching his response as I sought to help him understand the importance of partaking.

"We *want* the Lord Jesus to live inside us *all* the time, Son." He recognized the distinction between a moment's observance of a ritual and the continuing indwelling of a reality.

I was being careful, not wanting either to press beyond his ability to truly perceive or to push beyond the Holy Spirit's dimension of dealing with the young boy's heart. But it was

God's moment for Mark, and as He arranged it that way, everything merged into a precious, memorable experience for a dad.
My little boy really was saved that day! He really *did* understand,
and he really *did* receive Christ!

JESUS' SKIN?

The service had concluded now, and as I walked to the front of
the sanctuary to return the two cups, I invited Mark to walk with
me.

In our tradition, it is common for those who respond to an
evangelistic invitation to come forward for prayer and counseling. As we finished taking the bread and the cup, I had said to
Mark, "Now that you've received the Lord Jesus into your heart,
would you like to go up to the front and tell Dr. Duffield?" He
had smiled and brightly acknowledged his desire to do so, and
now we were there.

It was tenderly significant that this same man, who five years
before had held Mark in his arms and presented him to the Lord
in dedication as Anna and I brought our baby before the congregation, was about to hear of another birth. He had just finished exchanging remarks with one of the congregation and
then turned to us.

"Good morning, Jack." Then, grinning, he said, "How are
you, Mark? Did you have a nice Christmas?"

Mark responded with a child's usual bashfulness, and I lifted him up on the altar rail, so he could speak face to face with
the pastor.

I handed Dr. Duffield the two Communion cups, explaining, "We just had a very special time at Communion, and Mark
wanted to tell you what happened."

"Son," I said, turning to him, "tell Dr. Duffield what you did a few minutes ago."

The small boy straightened and with crystal clarity in his eyes, looked into the face of the older man. Then, with a singular certainty that only the Holy Spirit can bring to *any* heart—a child's as well—he said, "I asked Jesus to come into my heart."

Dr. Duffield was genuine in his joy. "Mark, that's wonderful! I'm so glad for that." His responsiveness clearly showed my son that his decision was as credible as any adult's. "I'm so happy you came to tell me." Then with gentle pastoral sensitivity, he took the boy's hand and offered a prayer of thanksgiving and assurance.

When we had finished, I thought I'd quiz Mark to let him show how well he knew what the elements of the Communion table represented. Taking a piece of broken bread from one of the trays at the table nearby, I gave it to him and asked, "Can you tell Dr. Duffield what this stands for?" His answer has become a classic family story, and it disrupted any possibility of sanctimony residing in the moment.

"This is Jesus' *skin!*"

Dr. Duffield and I exploded in laughter, our amusement sparked by Mark's choice of terms. But I explained the difference between body and skin to Mark, and then we said good-bye. Taking my son's hand, I started up the aisle thinking how grateful I was— so thankful to be part of a church that worshiped with power and which also kept Communion's meaning before its people.

A LOST FOCUS

"In Remembrance of Me" is carved into the front of a million tables in a million sanctuaries around the world, the Lord's Table being the most thoroughly established tradition on this planet. In terms of the frequency of its observance and the sheer number who participate in it, Communion doesn't have a vital counterpart anywhere. If there is any single, central point of Christian worship, it's the Lord's Table. It is also a central point of needed reform because of a common problem of lost focus in its observance.

When Jesus said "Do this in remembrance of Me," He obviously was addressing the human inclination to forget, but what He wanted us to remember is not as obvious nor is it as well defined. I'm convinced that much of the Church has a reverse view on the central point of Jesus' command, and the difference is between *life* and *death*.

Of course, any lost focus isn't due to a lack of intelligence. There are greater minds than mine presiding over the Table at many locations in the Church. But I do feel that a preoccupation with the details of the history of Jesus' passion supplants His intent—that we remember the *victory* He won. I think a new reformation needs to impact the mood of our celebration, and that can only precipitate from a fresh assessment of Christ's meaning in instituting Communion. I will answer these questions later, but let me stir thought with them as a starting place:

1. What does Christ want remembered at His Table?
2. How best can "thanksgiving" (the meaning of *eucharist*) be practiced?
3. What mood ought to characterize the receiving of Communion?
4. How can the *worship* at Christ's Table become a *witness* of His power?

A good beginning for any reform at the Lord's Table might be in our studying the first reform ever applied to it. It wasn't in

Europe in the sixteenth century but in Corinth in the first. The issue then was also one of lost focus, and a look at Paul's dealing with the Corinthians provides very workable insights for worshiping at the Lord's Table today:

> Now in giving these instructions I do not praise you, since you come together not for the better but for the worse. For first of all, when you come together as a church, I hear that there are divisions among you, and in part I believe it. For there must also be factions among you, that those who are approved may be recognized among you. Therefore when you come together in one place, it is not to eat the Lord's Supper. For in eating, each one takes his own supper ahead of others; and one is hungry and another is drunk. What! Do you not have houses to eat and drink in? Or do you despise the church of God and shame those who have nothing? What shall I say to you? Shall I praise you in this? I do not praise you (1 Cor. 11:17-22).

The people in Corinth had become confused about a number of matters concerning the believer's lifestyle and worship. Since the Lord's Table is so central to New Testament worship, it's not surprising that they needed correction there, too. The apostle's approach to their many problems was consistently direct and patient. In writing to correct and adjust, he acknowledges their unusual vulnerability to confusion by reason of their past: "Remember how you were when you didn't know God, led from one phony god to another" (1 Cor. 12:2, THE MESSAGE). Their background had colored and altered several foundational aspects of their corporate life as believers and the Lord's Table was just one example: Communion time had become party time.

One might first question how so meaningful an observance as the Lord's Table could ever have become so warped. Their now confused practice, which Paul claims to have originally introduced them to in a pure form, had become a cross between a picnic and a social spree. The context shows that some worshipers were being completely left out, while others were feasting as though invitations read, "B.Y.O.D.—Bring Your Own Dinner! If you don't have it with you, you won't get any from me!" The event had degenerated into some kind of bizarre banquet rather than a memorial to Jesus Christ. The Corinthians had obviously forgotten at least one thing they were supposed to remember: Christ's Body is *one*. Not only had irreverence taken over at the Table, but also disunity and selfishness. Incredible!

In 1 Corinthians 11:21,22, Paul directs people to eat at home to answer hunger's basic need and to observe the Lord's Table with smaller, representative portions. Paul had to cool what had become wild enthusiasm and correct what had become rampant self-centeredness.

Apostolic correction in this situation was very necessary, of course, but it seems that even to this day a residue of reticence lingers around anything Paul corrected in Corinth. If they exaggerated it, it seems the assignment in our time is to underplay it. The degree to which we fear being "Corinthian" is not so much reflected in our balance as in our tendency to run toward equally exaggerated and opposite extremes. For example, it has become traditional in the Church to scorn fornicators rather than to scold and then restore them. And it is widely deemed more acceptable to skip the "tongues" altogether than to venture the possibility. Corinthian ignorance on a given theme seems to breed contemporary ignoring of the same. This pattern holds for the Church's contemporary approach to the Lord's Table.

The remedial action Paul took against the Corinthians' fool-ish extremes seems to have been interpreted down through the ages as outright insistence that Communion always be observed with cool reserve. Our reaction to the confusion in Corinth has bred a Churchwide reluctance to *celebrate* in the partaking of Communion. It's rare that we see actual rejoicing at the Lord's Table. Forthright praise or a plain show of human joyfulness tends to be interpreted as potentially irreverent—risky of a recur-rence of Corinthian excess. Far too often, what Jesus left as the Church's "thanksgiving dinner" is more of a postfuneral buffet. Rather than celebrating a victory, something of a pall hangs over the Table.

But Communion is a harvest-time celebration!

Jesus was sown as a seed-unto-death and has been raised again as the Firstfruits of resurrection-life triumph! Yet instead of our celebrating a harvest of life, our observances often seem more like the gathering of loved ones at a postinterment recep-tion, where it is customary for family members to speak in hushed tones of the one just buried. Peculiarly enough, Communion is often "celebrated" in this same heaviness of spir-it, a practice which has virtually been sanctified as though it were the essence of reverence.

I propose that the Corinthians' loss of focus is not lacking a contemporary parallel. However, where theirs was a loss of per-spective on reverence, I think ours has become a misinterpreta-tion of it. Joy, triumph and a visitation of divine power hardly seem allowable, and yet the celebration of Christ's cross ought to occasion the preaching of all three—with a presiding spirit of victory!

To what degree we may need a reformation in worship at the Lord's Table might be evidenced with some self-analysis. Ask yourself these questions:

- Do I find the music employed at Communion to be always subdued if not dirgelike?
- Have I noticed that an unnatural somberness prevails over the serving of the Lord's Table?
- Has something of an exaggerated concern for the machinelike distribution of the elements become more important than a sense of a corporate partaking together—reducing to private activity what is ideally an occasion of being gathered for power?
- Does the occasion ever seem to breed guilt rather than release deliverance?
- Have I ever witnessed the Table being made a battleground of separation, rather than holy ground where an invitation to life, forgiveness and unity is issued?

VERBAL OR VITAL?

What is it Christ wants to have remembered at His Table?

We know the *verbal* answer: *Him.* He said, "Do this in remembrance of *Me*" (Luke 22:19, emphasis mine). But the verbal answer is not the same as the *vital* answer, and it in no way automatically ensures our grasping the real point in Communion. If we can receive them, I believe Paul's words zero in on precisely what Jesus had in mind:

> As often as you eat this bread and drink this cup, *you proclaim the Lord's death* till He comes (1 Cor. 11:26, emphasis mine).

What is Paul proposing here? That we retell the story of the Crucifixion? That we reenact the suffering He underwent? Or are we to declare the fruit of His death? On the surface of the

LET US ONCE
AGAIN ENJOY
THE LORD'S
TABLE AS A
POSITIVE,
REVERENTLY
REJOICING,
POWER-FILLED
CELEBRATION
OF THE CROSS!

mere words it could appear that "Don't forget Jesus' death" meant a solemn, ritual review of the events on Calvary. But I think reason recommends that Christ meant us to observe more than a morbid, funereal, commemorative service.

I don't think anything like that ever existed in any first-century congregation. If a commemoration of death was what Jesus had in mind and if that's what the Early Church celebrated, then there can be no rational explanation for how the Corinthians ever arrived at so exaggerated a feast.

However, if early believers celebrated Christ's death with joy, remembering the Cross as the God-given key to life, then it becomes plausible that a carnal, pagan-just-turned-Christian community might have distorted so joyous a feast. If Paul had instituted a somber, contemplative observance of the Table, it seems unlikely that the festivities could have so evolved. However, if under Paul's founding pastoral leadership the Corinthians had been led to the Lord's Table as an occasion for remembering the triumph of the Cross,

the power of its provision and

the joy of our hope,

and if the celebration were focused on what Jesus *finished* for us at Calvary, then a disposition toward feasting becomes understandable. It is then imaginable, with the passage of the five years between Paul's pastorate in Corinth and his first epistle to them, that a young church newly birthed out of a bacchanalian culture might lose its balance.

I propose that the Early Church celebrated the Table as a positive, pointed, reverently rejoicing, power-filled celebration of the Cross. Even though it might have deteriorated into a self-centered feast in Corinth, I doubt Paul—or God!—ever intended the pendulum to swing to the other extreme. Generally speaking, I believe a reformation in worship needs to come to the Lord's Table and shake off the shackles of suffocating morbidity.

We need to define more specifically the reason for the Lord Jesus' concern that we remember Him. This is more crucial than some may suppose, because a funereal approach to Christ's Table is not only depressing, but it also almost suggests a neurotic's self-centeredness in Jesus' words "Remember Me"—an appeal that would be unworthy of anyone, much less the Son of God.

To observe the mood of some Communion services I've conducted in the past, one would think the object was to pacify a God who was still irritated that we caused Him so much inconvenience and injury. Ask yourself: *In commanding, "Remember Me," did Jesus mean to direct us to periodically commiserate together and remember how badly the cross hurt Him? Did He mean to call us to His Table to ceaselessly hound us: "Remember, it's your fault I had to go through all this, and I don't want you to ever forget it!"?*

Have you ever witnessed Communion observances that seemed more geared to self-flagellation than holy celebration? What can be done?

RESTORING OUR FOCUS

To begin, let's help worshipers distinguish the difference between somberness and sobriety. The two are often blurred, somewhat the same way as reverence has been made synonymous with silence. The somberness often dominating Communion is depressing, while a healthy sobriety of heart can be discerning; the latter is appropriate, but one questions if the former *ever* is.

Of course, there will be occasions more subdued than others. For example, our Good Friday services usually include the entire recounting of Jesus' death and suffering. Such a sensitive annual commemoration is certainly appropriate and desirable. I personally observe a three-day fast leading up to Good Friday every year, essentially as a means of helping me remember Jesus' passion for me. I do believe a sensible soul will periodically reflect on the physical agony and emotional anguish Jesus experienced for us in giving His life. But in the main, it seems difficult to suppose Jesus ever meant our regular Communion remembrance to focus on His agony in a way that would instill guilt in our souls in an atmosphere of defeat. We surely must *never* take His suffering lightly, for the Cross was a grotesque, torturous event, but remembering Him doesn't require reliving its horror.

I submit that biblical evidence reveals that Jesus' "Remember Me" calls for a victorious, regular remembrance focused on the accomplishments of His cross. I propose that

Paul, in directing us to "proclaim the Lord's death until He comes," meant the proclamation to be the same good news Jesus announced. In His own ministry, Calvary has obtained and accentuated the ongoing availability of this message of hope and promise:

> The Spirit of the Lord is upon Me, because He has anointed Me to preach the gospel to the poor . . . to heal the brokenhearted . . . to proclaim liberty to the captives . . . and recovery of sight to the blind . . . to set at liberty those who are oppressed (Luke 4:18).

Isn't it more likely that if Jesus were to preside next Sunday at His Table where we worship, He would say: "While you're partaking, I want you to remember what I've secured for you. I want you . . .

- to enjoy every benefit of forgiveness,
- to receive every provision of victory,
- to enter into freedom from every point of bondage and
- partake of My healing presence and power!"

Of course He doesn't want us to forget!

Of course He would say "Remember!" He suffered death to make it all possible, and His Table is His way of keeping the provisions of Calvary constantly before us. Our Great Shepherd has prepared a table before us in the presence of our enemies, and He invites us to it in order to anoint our heads with oil that our cup of rejoicing may overflow (see Ps. 23:5).

We are not serving a neurotic Savior who summons our nostalgia. To urge the spirit of celebration at His Table is not to suggest we are becoming casual about Calvary. On the contrary, we come to His Table with joy to exalt His name for His massive victory there. Any residue of a medieval mind-set of morbidity and false reverence deserves to be removed from Christ's Table and a holy celebration reinstituted. To point the way, I propose these answers to the questions presented earlier in this chapter. Maybe they can constitute a focal point helping us remember what I think Jesus meant us to remember.

Q.   *What does Christ want remembered at His Table?*

A.   He wants us to remember that through the Cross a complete accomplishment was made of His perfect work of salvation, including:

- *Full justification* for every believer, rendering each of us not only as forgiven but also causing each of us to be regarded in Christ as never having sinned at all (see Rom. 3:23-26; 4:23—5:2; 8:1,2).
- *Full dominion* over all the powers of hell, rendering every bond of soul or spirit broken and bringing deliverance now from every hellish affliction (see Eph. 1:18-23; 4:7,8; Col. 2:13-15).
- *Full availability* of healing for every dimension of our personality, seeing that through His suffering, by His stripes, we *are* healed (see Isa. 53:5; Matt. 8:17; 1 Pet. 2:24).
- *Full release* of God's love, poured forth by His Spirit to fill our souls with peace and to bring reconciling peace and restored unity to strained human relationships (see Rom. 5:5; 2 Cor. 5:15-21; Eph. 2:14-17).

Q.   *How best can "thanksgiving" (the meaning of eucharist) be practiced?*

A. Thanksgiving can best be displayed by a prevailing spirit of praise characterizing the worship we bring to the Lord's Table. This does not recommend or require a giddiness, lightness or irreverence. It does require a reassessment of tradition and an alteration of any of the morbid, funereal or dirgelike habits we have unwittingly allowed to surround our worship at Communion.

Q. *What mood ought to characterize the receiving of Communion?*
A. A mood of expectancy, based on a clear-eyed commemoration of the primary fact central to the Communion table: the meaning and achievement of His death! In our remembrance of His dying once for all, Christ has not called us to reenact His death but to remember His triumph. "It is finished!" was not a whimpered cry. It is the call from Calvary that echoes across the centuries, down the corridors of hell and throughout the ramparts of heaven! Jesus is both Lord and Conqueror, and each time we come to His Table we need to remember *that* and allow faith to fill our hearts for every need we have or circumstance we face!

Q. *How can the worship at Christ's Table become a witness of His power?*
A. Worship *and* witness can fill our time at Christ's Table by our employing the observance as an opportunity to apply the provisions of Calvary, not simply to remember them. The biblical word "proclaim" underscores a *ministering* of the memorial, not merely an observance thereof. Perhaps this might most be exemplified in the possibilities of seeing people brought to Christ by inviting them to His feast.

A TABLETIME INVITATION

We have found Communion worship to be an ideal time for evangelism. That was foreign to my upbringing, and it took a reformation of sorts to release me into such ministry as our "tabletime invitation."

First, let me say and emphasize that I feel keenly about and have always been cautious about inviting any "as yet" unbelievers to Christ's Table (see 1 Cor. 11:29). However, I began doing it, notwithstanding my caution, because no matter how much I studied the Scriptures, I couldn't find anything prohibiting an unbeliever being invited to the Table.

Once I did that, I found many being born again there. My predisposition had been against the possibility of opening Christ's Table to too wide a participation. I had grown somehow to see myself as the Table's guardian against unworthy intruders. Any suggestion of an open table was reckless if not heretical, but an important line of discernment changed my perspective.

I began to recognize the vast difference between a sacrilegious person and a searching one—between the indifferent and the inquiring. I became convinced that Jesus would invite the searching heart to partake at His Table, for His own lifestyle and parables support an outreaching viewpoint. He ate with publicans and sinners, never compromising, but ever reaching to them. His parabolic teaching also indicated a wide-openness in God's heart, inviting people to His salvation feast: "Come, for all things are ready—go out and compel the needy to come in" (see Matt. 22:4; Mark 2:16; Luke 14:23).

As a result of becoming convinced away from my tradition-fixed fears through a fresh exposure to God's Word, I began to preface our congregation's corporate times of Communion like this:

"As we come to the Lord's Table today, I want to invite *everyone* who is here to partake with us. Indeed, I want to *urge* you to do so, just as surely as if you were at our house at dinnertime.

"It would be impolite to not invite you at least. However, we're not merely being polite; we honestly are wanting you to share with us. Whatever your religious background or absence of one, you needn't hesitate—you're welcome here. We refuse to close this Table to anyone, because, in fact, it isn't ours.

"This Table is Christ's. He is the One who provided this feast—a feast of forgiveness. He did it when He died to open salvation to us all, and He's the One who calls us all to come here and remember that. His Word is clear: Whosoever will may come (see Matt. 11:28-30; John 3:16,17; Rev. 22:17).

"I think it is obvious that it would be meaningless and therefore wrong for anyone to partake disrespectfully or indifferently. But barring that, let me urge you to come with us. Let us come and thank God for the gift of His Son, and thank His Son for the gift of His life for us."

With such an approach to Communion worship, the witness of Jesus' love, life and power fills the room. At some point during the actual time of partaking, I will invite those who "even now are opening your lives toward Jesus" to make a firm decision. It is no wonder that almost every time we worship at the Lord's Table, there are several first-time respondents who acknowledge Jesus Christ as Savior. Following this, an opportunity is given to proceed to the prayer room for counseling and they *do* go—these who actually made their decision *during* the time that they were partaking with us.

Our invitation to the unsaved is only one way that His Table may bear *witness*. Healing and affirmation are also dynamic possibilities.

The witness of Christ's healing power can be extended in simple faith by allowing believers to obey Jesus' directive: "They will lay hands on the sick, and they will recover" (Mark 16:18). Often when the bread is being partaken, we will pause and restate the verse: "This is my body that is broken for you," noting that Jesus said His physical suffering was specifically *for* us—that is, in our interest. Just as He died to save us from our sin, He also suffered to obtain and provide relief from our multiplied afflictions.

On these grounds, I encourage worshipers simply to lift a hand to indicate their desire to have nearby worshipers lay hands upon them in Jesus' name. It is done without ostentation or religious pomp, as a very brief time is allowed for those who surround each petitioner to pray over him or her. The results are remarkable, and there are regular testimonies of healing which flow from this practice.

And what a time to love one another!

This is the heart of our witness to the world—the unity of the Body living in the Spirit of Jesus Himself. We nearly always conclude our Communion service by rising together, taking time to embrace those around us and affirm one another in the love and joy of Christ. There is a religious resistance to hugging in church, but this also needs to be reformed in the light of God's Word. There are no less than five New Testament epistles that *command* all believers to "greet one another with a holy kiss" (Rom. 16:16; 1 Cor. 16:20; see also 2 Cor. 13:12; 1 Thess. 5:26; 1 Pet. 5:14). The term "kiss" is appropriately translated to embrace and therefore a hug is an appropriate counterpart.

The marvel of such meetings as these at His Table is that an electric sense of victory, healing, love and deliverance fills the room. If the worship of Jesus is central, nothing of irreverence or silliness can creep in. No one is in any danger of forgetting either the price of the Cross or what it purchased. These moments of memorial have been given to remembering what Jesus wanted to be remembered—and His people are fed at His Table of triumph.

* * * * *

That was the spirit of the meeting the day Mark was born again.

A five-year-old boy understood and though it was his dad who gave the explanation on that occasion, whenever God's people understand and communicate Christ's victory, there will be a fresh experience of the same. They will learn again what it means to be a part of His Church, overcoming "by the blood of the Lamb and by the word of their testimony" (Rev. 12:11).

By reason of his limited experience, my young son had used the word "skin" instead of "body," and his imprecision in terms had brought a chuckle to a pair of adults. But in another sense, maybe we adults need more of Jesus' "skin" in Communion. One wonders if Christ Himself isn't desirous of a reformation in our worship at His Table, one which will let Him "put skin on" His manifest victory by proclaiming that triumph again and again, through and among His people who celebrate that victory *here and now!*

CHAPTER 14

HIS MAJESTY SPEAKS

Behold, I make all things new! Believe it, for My words all are true.
And that truth can bring you into liberty—Behold, I make all things new!

There is no reason to doubt the man's testimony. He had proven trustworthy throughout many years of fellowship and service. But when someone claims to have seen visions, well, it may understandably make any of us cautious. And if he tells you he saw Jesus, I suppose we all would confess to at least a momentary twinge of skepticism.

But that's exactly what the man said: "I saw Jesus." He told it this way.

"As you know, vicious and agonizing persecution of Christians had come to our area, and as a result of my stand for Jesus Christ, I was sent to an island penal colony—this particular gulag being not more than 100 miles from my home.

"I had been there for several weeks, feeling nothing unusual other than the loneliness, the lurking sense of depression I suppose any prisoner feels. On this particular day, the guards had allowed us a period of reprieve from our routine of labor, and I had wandered alone to a secluded spot. I sat down on a large stone, facing the sea to the west, the surrounding rocks creating something of a small, chapel-like formation behind me. I was completely without expectation or preparation for what happened, for suddenly I heard a voice. It was so loud I was literally shaken, totally removed from anything approximating a reverie—and that's how I know I wasn't in a trance of some kind. The voice fairly shouted:

> There is nothing that precedes Me and nothing beyond Me! I have always been and will be when time no longer exists. I am here to remove your fears of the future, for I too have been through the pangs of death and the horrors of hell, and I'm here to tell you: All will be well!

"I was stunned, and even while He was speaking I began to turn around. What I saw exceeds description, for even though I knew it was Jesus, I could not have imagined nor can I adequately describe the marvelously transcendent glory of His appearance. Only one word can begin it: *Majestic!*

"His whole being seemed to be infused with light—perhaps *fire* is the better way to state it. A regal garment that seemed to be woven of gold draped to His feet—feet that I can't forget, for though they were without shoes, they shone with an unearthly brilliance. I was surprised that His hair was white, but it wasn't gray as though dimmed by age; it was sheened as though silvered with glory.

"The eyes were unforgettable. They seemed as glowing coals, not of a smoldering, sinister quality, but emanating a warmth, a power and a penetrating purity of sight which reached into my being when He spoke."

From this point, the man continued his account of what Christ said to him, but insofar as the elements of his vision were concerned, that's what he said he saw. And now, having relayed his testimony to you, I wonder what your feeling is about it? I mean, can you accept it at all?

It's probably an unfair question. You're probably the same as I am in such regard. Even if we allow for the possibility of visions as being real and not imagined, we would both probably reserve judgment until we met the person claiming to have had one.

However, in this particular case, I think you've already passed judgment. I suppose you already believe it, for the report above is actually one you've probably read before in other terms. It was written less than 1,900 years ago, and the more commonly read version goes like this:

> I, John. . . . was in the Spirit on the Lord's Day, and I heard behind me a loud voice, as of a trumpet, saying, "I am the Alpha and the Omega. . . . Do not be afraid; I am the First and the Last. I am He who lives, and was dead, and behold, I am alive forevermore. Amen. And I have the keys of Hades and of Death. Write the things which you have seen, and the things which are, and the things which will take place after this" (Rev. 1:9-11,17-19).

The apostle John wrote these words on the Isle of Patmos where he was exiled by the imperial Roman government because of his leadership and influence for the gospel of Jesus Christ. His narrative of the vision he had of Jesus continues in the book of Revelation:

> Then I turned to see the voice that spoke with me. And having turned I saw seven golden lampstands, and in the midst of the seven lampstands One like the Son of Man, clothed with a garment down to the feet and girded about the chest with a golden band. His head and hair were white like wool, as white as snow, and His eyes like a flame of fire; His feet were like fine brass, as if refined in a furnace, and His voice as the sound of many waters; He had in His right hand seven stars, out of His mouth went a sharp two-edged sword, and His countenance was like the sun shining in its strength. And when I saw Him, I fell at His feet as dead. But He laid His right hand on me, saying to me, "Do not be afraid; I am the First and the Last" (Rev. 1:12-17).

A TWENTY-FIRST-CENTURY VISION OF JESUS CHRIST

There is a reason I have sought to lead you into John's vision by an apparent detour, as though relating to you some contemporary vision of Christ.

I've done it because I think we need it.

I think we need to be reminded that Jesus has been known to appear to people, to stir them afresh with a vision of the Church as it is and the Church as it can be.

I think we all need a twenty-first-century vision of Jesus Christ—at least in terms of hearing His call to a new era of conquest unveiled by a new encounter with Him in worship.

Is that credible to you? Or do our traditions disallow the expectation of our being impacted just as John was? Does it disturb you as it does me that I can comfortably read of John's personal encounter and be unmoved by its implications for me? That's why I think we need to experience our *own* vision.

When I say we need a vision, the object is not sensation-seeking, ecstasy or escapism. It's *confrontation*—a stark, raw, earth-quaking, staggering shake-up of our senses and our sensitivities through a fresh, brutally realistic encounter with the King—His Majesty, Jesus, Lord of the Church.

A literary excursion into rephrased history might briefly help us consider the possibility of such a vision, but the real and lasting way to meet and be met by Him is through a more certain and attainable means than seeking our own private visions.

That way is *worship*.

Worship rid of its tameness, its predictability, its numbing formality and its prisonlike presuppositions of propriety.

Such a total and complete upheaval as I need in my own soul

THE HOLY SPIRIT IS WAITING FOR HEARTS THAT HUNGER AND THIRST FOR HIM TO BRING AN UNPRECEDENTED VISITATION OF GOD TO OUR GENERATION.

will probably never allow for this encounter to take place in public—not because I fear being humbled before others, but because Jesus has a way of dealing with each of us so uniquely that a private setting becomes necessary.

The purpose of such an encounter (and the reason I invite you to join me in such a quest) is that the same realities lay hold of our souls just as they gripped John's:

The reality of Christ's majestic person.

The reality of Christ's authoritative position.

The reality of Christ's consummate power.

I am convinced the Holy Spirit is waiting for hearts that hunger and thirst for an unprecedented visitation of God to our generation, displaying His glorious power and might to every culture and in every church. And I am equally convinced that the one pathway to that visitation's taking place is a reformation in the worship life of the Church, just as dramatic and dynamic as the reformation in the theology of the Church was five centuries ago.

SEEING JESUS' PERSON

John saw Jesus as He is, the majestic, exalted, enthroned King. Each trait of His personality seems to be emblazoned in the very flesh and sinew of His glorified body that radiates regality and dominion.

I want to be a candidate to look into His eyes and be purified by that fire that waits to surge into me and purge all of me. I want to bow at His feet, not only to touch the marks of ancient wounds, but also to be reminded that their brasslike character declares His complete qualification to bring all principalities and powers beneath them.

I want to fall before Him, dead to my self and sin and alive to receive His transmission to me of His authority to minister it in His name.

I want Him to lay His right hand on me, just as He did John, and to so clearly speak His certainty of triumph into my soul that whatever trial, whatever test, whatever pain, whatever assault of hell I face—or however despondent, depressed or despairing I might become under duress of difficulty—I will be steeled against defeat and stand unshakable through His Word.

HEARING JESUS' VOICE

John also heard Jesus speak from His position as Lord of the Church, and I bow in His presence to hear those same words again.

- His message to Ephesus is His call to me: Come away from the deceptive supposition that doctrinal purity or diligent labor will ever substitute for passionate devotion. The timeless call to us is "Repent! Return to your first love!" (see Rev. 2:1-7).
- His message to Smyrna is His reminder that my wealth is neither now nor ever in my accumulation of material things but in that pure gold of character that flows out of the refining fires of struggle and tribulation—trial through which He guarantees to bring me if I will keep tuned to the Spirit's voice (see Rev. 2:8-11).
- His message to Pergamos and Thyatira is His insistence that I give no place to the sensuous and the seductive, which in every age will seek an avenue of justifying carnal indulgence and rationalizing sexual excesses (see Rev. 2:12-29).
- His message to Sardis is His commentary on the shallow human supposition that an established reputation

among mankind is in any way impressive to God. The qualifications for recognition on His terms are always the same: a continuously shapeable, teachable, hearing heart that walks in repentant response to the present word the Spirit is speaking to the Church, and a simple walk in faith which overcomes the spirit of the world (see Rev. 3:1-6).

- His message to Philadelphia is His constant encouragement to me, for He never forgets or overlooks my deep desire to please Him, and He promises to open doorways unto my next realm of victory—doors which once He opens, no power can resist (see Rev. 3:7-13)!
- His message to Laodicea is His agelong reminder of the vulnerability of my flesh to enshrine success as though gain were God. He calls me from the chilling effect of such blindness and promises to anoint my eyes, clothe my nakedness and refire my soul; and He promises to enter the open door of my welcome to Him (see Rev. 3:14-22). Come in and dine with me, Jesus.

Reformed worship is refired worship! It will bring us into Christ's presence to witness His Majesty, and it will bring us to His feet to acknowledge His Lordship.

EXPERIENCING JESUS' POWER

John's vision included one more thing: He saw the consummate power of Christ through to the end of all things. The whole book of Revelation unfolds the message that always and ever, consummately and ultimately, Jesus Christ is Lord and King! He is God triumphant!

And with that vision, one wonders if John were drawn back to another day—a day when the breezes flowing down from Hermon brought a rhythmic sway to the grasses so freshly garbing the Galilean hillsides that spring. The same settings which had witnessed such a magnificence of divine grace—the healings, the teachings, the deliverances, the recovery of the broken—all seemed relatively silent now. No crowds were present, but there was a small gathering of almost a dozen men who seemed to be reminiscing on golden moments of many months before.

Then, He came.

So simply did He arrive, not one of them could be sure if He had slipped up from the flank of their mountaintop situation—*Did He come from the grove of trees over there?*—or if He just appeared miraculously.

When they saw Him, they worshiped Him; but some doubted. And Jesus came and spoke to them, saying, "All authority has been given to Me in heaven and on earth. Go therefore and make disciples of all the nations, baptizing them . . . teaching them . . . and lo, I am with you always, even to the end of the age" (Matt. 28:17-20).

There's an ineffable glory to this moment, but there is also a distinctly plaintive tone to the text: "They worshiped . . . but some doubted."

Some doubted?

Yes . . . and sometimes so do we.

We need not belabor those men just being birthed into an age mankind could never have imagined. Their doubt occasioned no criticism by the Savior, for He understood the awesome transitions they were being called to accept—the overthrow of presuppositions about how Messiah's rule would be extended, as well as their call to open themselves to a new power source in the Holy Spirit being promised them. It was all so new . . . and some doubted.

But they worshiped.

Their dignity and the release of their destiny was that they worshiped—and so may it be with us. It was unto that worshiping band (in spite of those lingering doubts which shortly would be abolished) that Jesus did two things: He commissioned them *and* He conferred divine authority upon them.

All authority has been given to Me (Matt. 28:18).

But you shall receive power when the Holy Spirit has come upon you (Acts 1:8).

As the Father has sent Me, I also send you (John 20:21).

Go into all the world (Mark 16:15).

The realm of rule once lost by man was made potential again to the redeemed. Worshipers were made recipients of Kingdom authority at Pentecost, that they might be equipped to fulfill His Majesty's call to extend the dominion of His throne to every person possible until His return.

And, thus, we are called.

Whatever remains of the present age until He comes again, this much is clear: His Spirit is working newness today wherever open hearts are pliable. He no more requires our instant mastery of lingering doubt than He did those early apostles. He only calls us to worship, to offer up all glory, honor and praise.

For it is there, as we exalt and lift up on high the name of His Majesty, that doubts will be scattered like shadows.

For it is there that His power will be poured out like new wine and that Kingdom authority will flow to us.

For it is there that Jesus who died, now glorified, will be revealed among us.

So magnify, come glorify Jesus.

Worship His Majesty!

A THEOLOGY OF WORSHIP

The following summary has been used by the author for conducting seminars on worship and for directing interaction with visiting pastors at the Jack W. Hayford School of Pastoral Nurture, a division of The King's Seminary in Van Nuys, California.

An Outline for Thought and Discussion

1. As God above all, the Lord Almighty is our Creator, Sustainer, Redeemer and Deliver; and as the Sovereign of the universe, He is worthy of our worship and deserving of our praise.

2. As His creatures, we are called to worship (*a*) by the logic of our dependency upon Him, (*b*) by the glory of His exceeding beauty and goodness and (*c*) by the grace and love of His redeeming kindness toward us.

3. Despite these facts, it seems most Christian worship is approached as an academic duty-affirming faith through holy observance, rather than as a dynamic moment anticipating life through holy expectation.

4. The objective in our worship is not merely to fulfill a prerequisite acknowledging our place in the created order, but worship is a God-ordained means for advancing our restoration and reinstatement in that order.

5. Worship is God's gift to us for our blessing more than His. His objective is not the securing of our adulation but our discovery and realization of advancement in His intended purpose for our fulfillment.

6. Worship is not only a means of reaffirming man's relational dependence upon, submission to and obedience before God; but it is also the means (through grace) to the reinstatement of man's partnership with God in ruling the earth—one which begins in a present, practical, yet partial, realization, and will succeed after Christ's coming unto a complete and full realization.

7. For the redeemed, worship is the essential key to welcoming the rule of the kingdom of God into human experience—i.e., our daily affairs, our homes, our congregations, our business affairs and our cities and nations.

8. Thus, worship is the primary means for the establishing of an atmosphere (*a*) for the transforming entry of God's presence, (*b*) for the clear entry of God's Word, (*c*) for the loving entry of God's Spirit and (*d*) for the dynamic entry of God's works of power.

9. Accordingly, worship should be approached by the leadership with conviction that we are not providing an optional moment, but we are determining a pivotal moment.

10. With this understanding, we must confront the fact that biblical worship (*a*) will always require the humbling of human pride *through* worship, (*b*) must appropriately be conducted according to divine guidelines *for* worship and (*c*) will regularly manifest in the transforming joy and humility distilling *from* worship.

WORSHIP IN SPIRIT AND TRUTH

The following is adapted from an article by the author which first appeared in the Spring 1999 issue of Leadership *magazine and is reprinted here by permission.*

In my experience, theological discussions about worship tend to focus on the cerebral, not the visceral—on the mind, not the heart. True worship, we are often taught, is more about the mind's thinking right about God (using theologically correct language and liturgy), rather than the heart's hunger for Him.

But the words of our Savior resound the undeniable call to worship that transcends the intellect: "God is Spirit, and those who worship Him must worship in spirit and truth" (John 4:24).

We have been inclined to conclude that *mind* is the proper synonym for *spirit* here, but the Bible shows that the *heart* is a better candidate. The words "in truth" certainly suggest participation of the intellect in worship, but it inescapably comes second and is dependent upon the heart's fullest release first.

This priority is usually held suspect. The heart is said to be governed by affections and thus is more vulnerable to deception than is the intellect. But to base worship on our intellects is to entertain a dual delusion: first, that the mind is less subject to deception than the heart; second, that the mind is the main means to contact God in worship (note verses like Job 11:7: "Can you search out the deep things of God?").

Yes, human intelligence contributes to our worship, but God's Word indicates He is not looking for something brilliant but something broken:

> The sacrifices of God are a broken spirit, a broken and
> a contrite heart—these, O God, You will not despise (Ps.
> 51:17).

The exercises of our enlightened minds may deduce God, but only our ignited hearts can delight Him—and in turn experience His desire to delight us!

How God Evaluates Worship

To be more specific, I believe that to please God, worship must do four things:

1. True Worship Treasures God's Presence.

God welcomes those into His presence who want Him. The

quest may be one of desperation or of delight, of frantic need or of loving hunger for fellowship, but the motivation is clear—and so is His pleasure with it.

In Exodus 33 and 34, a tender and powerful exchange takes place between God and Moses, spanning the emotional range from an intimate face-to-face encounter to a dramatic declaration by the Almighty. But central to the encounter is the cry of Moses: "Now therefore, I pray, if I have found grace in Your sight, show me now Your way, that I may know You and that I may find grace in Your sight" (Exod. 33:13).

To which God replies, "My Presence will go with you, and I will give you rest" (v. 14).

Shortly following this, God displays His glory to Moses—as sure a sign of His pleasure and presence as He ever gives (see Exod. 40:33-38).

I had been in pastoral leadership for nearly 15 years when my thinking about corporate worship was transformed. Rather than tightly regimented gatherings concerned with aesthetics, mechanics and academic theology, we began to provide an unpressured portion of the service for free-flowing songs of praise and adoration. Within two years, our church began to experience God's glory and grace in new and more profound ways, an experience that continues to this day.

We've been vigilant in seeking constant renewal of the practice because we know that even the finest spiritual habits are vulnerable to the arthritis of ritualism—the point at which form loses its focus. But with gentleness, the Holy Spirit has a way of drawing us back to our "first love" (Rev. 2:4)—to a renewed hunger and thirst for the Living God.

Such worship encourages people to fall in love with God. If the phrase "fall in love" offends anyone (as it once did me—it wasn't sufficiently objective), perhaps we might learn to be equally offended by "reason" that distances the heart from a passion to simply know and love God.

2. True Worship Humbles the Heart.

In Isaiah 6:1-8, the abject cry of a sinful man, "Woe is me, for I am undone," was not an achievement of intellectual analysis but of self-discovery made upon entering God's presence.

Isaiah says "I saw the Lord" with neither apology nor arrogance; it was a breakthrough of grace that produced a breakup of pride. Isaiah, a member of the cultural, educated elite of Judah, demonstrates a childlike humility and teachability in this passage. His cry, without a vestige of style consciousness, reveals an unreserved availability to God.

This is the very thing to which Jesus calls us all:

Assuredly, I say to you, unless you are converted and become as little children, you will by no means enter the kingdom of heaven. Take heed that you do not despise one of these little ones, for I say to you that in heaven their angels always see the face of My Father who is in heaven (Matt. 18:3,10).

Because of the importance of humility, years ago I began encouraging people to become more expressive, both vocally and physically, in worship. Few things challenge our pride more than the simplest summons to expressiveness. I carry no brief for orchestrated calisthenics in church, as though a set of exercises made for superior liturgy. But I have learned that careful teaching and modeling can help people move beyond self-consciousness (and challenge the adult preoccupation with self-importance) so that they can experience a childlike liberty in expressing themselves in worship.

One of our members, with the best of motives, once suggested, "Pastor, if you didn't teach and invite people to lift their hands in worship, I think our church would grow faster," and then added, "I think you might injure some people's pride."

"*Injure* pride?" I said gently. "Why, I was hoping to kill it altogether."

I want to respect human dignity, but there is such a disposition—ensconced in the Church as surely as in the world—that equates dignity and pride. This is a *false* equation. It is because I value each individual in my congregation that I teach and model a way for us to come as children before the Father. Because pride tends to insist on finding a way to justify and preserve itself (even in church), I try to help people learn the humility of Isaiah. Only this will help them view God afresh and pave the way to deeply felt confession and purification.

3. True Worship Sacrifices and Then Expects Something from God.

Hebrews 11:6 puts it clearly: "He who comes to God must believe that He is, and that He is a rewarder of those who diligently seek Him." The text presupposes that worship always brings a sacrifice to God—that he who comes to the throne, whether with praise, with an offering or by "laying down" something instructed by the Holy Spirit, is presenting something of himself to God.

Simultaneously, we are told that the worshiper is to believe something will be given in return by God Himself—something rewarding, benevolent and good.

Some try to defend God against human selfishness and refuse all talk of reward. But the truth is, God freely offers the reward of His blessing—and delights to do so. He doesn't grouse, "Don't you dare give Me something and suppose you are manipulating Me to give it back!" Instead, His Word simply says, in effect, "Since you come to Me, I would expect you to believe I will reward your quest."

Of course, tithes or offerings (which are appropriate and biblical "sacrifices") aren't to be a tit-for-tat bargain with God! But God's call to worship is attended by His own commitment to bless us. The promise of God in Malachi 3:10 ("Try Me now in this . . . if I will not open for you the windows of heaven and pour out for you such blessing that there will not be room enough to receive it") reveals a largeness in the heart of God toward human giving—and the justice of our expecting a blessing in return.

Worship is God's gift to us, intended for our blessing and benefit. He doesn't need it; we do.

4. True Worship Extends God's Love.

If God-pleasing worship addresses human need, it also will extend God's love to others. It is therefore unsurprising that the greatest commandment issues into the second, which "is like it" in importance (see Matt. 22:38,39). The vertical mandate, to love and worship God, is also horizontal, to love our neighbor. This means such things as

- Forgiving others, seeking peace and reconciliation day by day
- Gracious lifestyle evangelism in both conduct and communication, living out a believable, winsome witness
- Unselfish, servant-minded attitude in assisting others in need, including a heart to care for victims of neglect and injustice

This need for us to reach out drives the prayer circles we have in nearly every worship service at our church. "Ministrytime,"

the formal name, lasts about 10 minutes as the people are directed to form small groups, share their needs and then pray. This
practice is essential to our effectiveness as a congregation.

Ministrytime accomplishes four things:

1. It is a pragmatic way to express God's love evoked during worship.
2. It helps people use their ministry gifts in the assembly.
3. It allows people to express themselves personally and
   to care and pray for one another.
4. It lays the foundation for the invitation—it is infinitely easier to invite people to receive the love of God in
   Jesus Christ after they have had a personal encounter
   with some people who have shown it!

What is birthed in the heart, then, finds expression in the
hands—hands that rise in humble praise, give in simple
expectancy and serve with gentle grace.

With such sacrifices, God seems to be well pleased.

LEADING WORSHIP IN THE NEW MILLENNIUM

The following is adapted from an address delivered by the author to the International Worship Institute in Dallas, Texas, on July 16, 1999.

As we begin a new millennium, I am filled with great hope and expectation for new dimensions of Kingdom life to flow from the Church of Jesus Christ. At this same juncture I have concerns in regard to the place where much of these new developments and growth will originate—in the worship life and leadership of the Church. When I say concerns, I'm not intending criticism, and I want to be deliberate at the outset to differentiate between the two. My concern and analysis are for the purpose of assisting today's worship leader toward a correction or improvement and not to beat anyone over the head with harsh and harmful criticism.

THE FOCUS OF THE WORSHIP LEADER

Worship leaders are not merely enjoying their own worship experience "on stage" as a demonstration and example; *they are leading people into the presence of God.*

When I lead a congregation in worship, I am not being insincere or simply going through the motions, but I have *had* my personal time of worship *before* I get on the platform. If a leader becomes lost in a personal time of worship, the leader isn't really able to lead. The leader must be keenly aware of (1) the response of the congregation, (2) the level of their response and (3) what should be done to lead them to the next stage of the process for the progress of the meeting.

The worship leader shepherds the people. I have watched inexperienced yet sincere leaders become lost in worship. You may be asking, "Isn't that what we should do?" My reply is a definitive "No." Shepherds do not go out to lead the sheep and marvel at their surroundings, enjoying the pastoral experience while losing track of the sheep. On the flip side, a leader can become overly conscious of the people, not for the sake of leading them into the presence of God, but because of self-consciousness. I vividly remember when the Lord confronted and exposed this self-consciousness in my own life.

The year was 1951 and I was playing in a band at our church in Oakland, California. We had really nice uniforms and everything about the band was really sharp and professional. I played the vibraphone, an instrument with pedals and golden keys similar to a xylophone. It's a beautiful instrument that isn't used much anymore.

On Sunday nights our congregation hosted huge evangelistic services and usually 20 to 25 people would receive the Lord. In the early part of the service, there was a time of singing old-time gospel hymns and I would play the "vibes," moving the pedal and changing the chords. The nature of the instrument requires considerable movement by the player, so I was one of the most visible members of the band along with the song leader and trumpet player. I was very conscious of this and it was heady stuff—and I knew that I was looking good. I had been raised to be careful and cautious to guard against that sort of pride, but I had become blinded to it.

As the band gathered to pray in one of the ministry rooms before one Sunday night service, the Holy Spirit slammed me right in the gut with the revelation: *You're more excited about going out there for the way you look than you are for what you're going to minister.* The band went out, but even though I knew my absence would leave a gaping hole on the platform, I didn't go with them.

Nobody noticed I wasn't going and while they were taking their places on the platform, I got on my knees and began to weep. I said, "Lord, I never want that to happen." I repented for the pride that had overtaken me and was heartbroken over the self-consciousness that had supplanted my ability to lead people in worship. I did not know then that the original worship leader in heaven, Lucifer, had became so captivated by the splendor of his own achievement that he finally became an enemy of the

Lord and led rebellion against Him. I did not know how satanic my pride in worship was; I only knew it was wrong.

I could have pushed this confrontation aside, to deal with it at a later time, and attended to my responsibilities in the band. Yet this incident was so confronting and revealing that I remained in that prayer room, allowing the Lord to do a vital and necessary work.

You can rationalize anything you want, any way you want and end up justifying whatever you wish; but if you do this, you will fail to confront the pride that will lead to eventual rebellion if left unchecked. Worship leaders are extremely vulnerable in this area, for they lead the people before the throne of God and are the ones the Adversary would most like to oppose. God's throne was the focal point of Satan's rebellion, and while that battle has been won through the Cross, Satan continually wants to keep people from approaching the throne. Everyone involved in worship leadership has to come to terms with this spiritual challenge in one way or another.

Your problem may or may not be as severe as mine was and subsequently not require as much attitude shaping. However, please hear me: The subtlety, the conniving and the cleverness of the Adversary, along with the sinister devices that he will employ to get you preoccupied with yourself, are unending in their creative and imaginative ways. He is endless in the quest to distract and deter you in your ability to lead people in worship.

THE WORSHIP REPERTOIRE

I am concerned when I visit a church and hear nothing but songs written by the worship leader or by the congregation. If your worship repertoire is exclusive, comprising only songs composed by your congregation, then you are not mixing and interacting with the larger Body of Christ.

Praise God for the creative things that are birthed in your own congregation. Thank God for those choruses that bring freshness and life to your body. Often there is a prophetic quality to them and the Lord speaks to your congregation through your musicians and composers. That is a wonderful thing, but if that is all you do, you are failing to recognize the need to be open to what the Holy Spirit is saying in the realm of praise and worship in other parts of the Body of Christ.

Some may not want to open up to other worship songs and choruses due to dishonesty in their own heart over the fact that they are jealous those songs have broader circulation than their own. We mask our jealousy and exclusivity with good and noble endeavors such as advancing "our music" the Lord has given *us*. We should be excited, but we should not be exclusive, for it is one of the ways we begin to divorce ourselves from involvement with the larger Body of Christ.

STYLE AND PRODUCTION CONSCIOUSNESS

Style consciousness occurs when you become overly conscious of how good you are getting. It is both wonderful and legitimate to be happy and to rejoice in the increased excellence, beauty and substance of your worship and your worship team's capacity to lead the congregation. It is good and right to be improving and growing, and it is good to thank the Lord for these developments. However, when your positive response becomes something other than happy and thankful, you need to deal with it.

It's something that rises up within you internally and other people may not notice it. The Holy Spirit may reveal the unpleasant truth to you about your attitude as He did to me that Sunday night in 1951. If you remain open to His work in your life, He will communicate the truth to you.

This revelation may come to you at a time when you are apparently doing great things and when you start to run ahead of God's plan for promoting what He has given to your congregation.

People constantly send me books and CDs and I am grateful for and value each one. Many of these are produced and promoted by local churches, but as worthy and often worthwhile as these projects are, I feel a sense of caution when a church puts out its own cassette or CD. This is not because I don't think they are potentially wonderful resources for the larger Body of Christ. Oftentimes they are quite good and beneficial. Thankfully, we live in a day when it's relatively easy to produce a quality CD. I want to be the first to encourage you to do all that God puts on your heart to do. However, once you do, inevitably the temptation will be to put out another one. The first one was simply to bless and serve the Body of Christ. But with the next one you may begin to feel as if you want to make your mark so to speak on a larger scale, seeking out publishers or other means of promotion.

If the Lord intends for your ministry to go national, He will bless it and make it happen. However, it is probably more likely that the worship songs and choruses God gave you were for your own local congregation. Once you start thinking "national" there comes a consuming desire to increase the quality of production, and you may begin to lose the sense of simplicity and spontaneity of what God gave you.

I am really concerned because I have watched this happen. We have never produced a worship album exclusively comprising material from our own congregation at The Church On The Way, even though some of the finest musicians, singers and instrumentalists in the Body of Christ attend our church. The only worship recordings we produce are cassettes of the songs we sang last month as a congregation. On these tapes the voices of the congregation are louder than that of the worship leader. These are "live" recordings without enhancements, and if the people listening to them have any taste for or knowledge of production quality, they likely would remark on how unremarkable it is. However, these tapes are not intended to be remarkable or to be widely distributed.

I have no argument against quality production, and I don't want to discourage anyone; but I do want to urge you not to lose sight of what God wants to do in your congregation because you are preoccupied with reaching a larger audience.

IN PRAISE OF HYMNS

I want to talk about hymns. By broaching this subject I run the risk of sounding old and antiquated, for when you mention hymns, people sometimes hearken back to days gone by with fond remembrance—while others think, *Good riddance!*

I am not lobbying for a return to hymnals, but I think we probably could all afford to have one at home for our private devotions. Frankly, it would be great if everyone in the Body of Christ had a hymnal at home, whether or not it was ever sung from. There is a treasure trove of substance, wealth and truth contained in these hymns, waiting to be rediscovered and pondered during devotional times. The verses and choruses have greater depth and insight than much of contemporary worship music.

For example, "A Mighty Fortress Is Our God" is a hymn with great meaning and spiritual insight, yet it is not often sung today. A couple of years ago, Tommy Walker rearranged this hymn for a Promise Keepers' rally. Stadiums across this country were suddenly filled with men singing this hymn and declaring the truth it contains. There are profound implications when the Church of today links with the Church of yesterday, singing hymns born out of past revivals and continuing what has been vital in the life of the Church.

Every hymn written is an expression of revival. In our modern age we must be careful not to discard these rich and beautiful lyrics in our effort to break free from dead tradition. I encourage you to tap in to the spirit of revival these hymns were birthed from, to write new melodies for the lyrics to update the style and transfer the wealth of these hymns to this generation of the Church. The term "hymn" refers to the lyric and technically the hymn is not the melody. In fact, if you look through old hymnals, you will notice a number of hymns that are written to the same melody; therefore, the updating of the melody of the hymn is not a departure from an essential quality of hymnology.

As a young pastor and composer I was challenged to compose a hymn. It was 1962 and Cliff Barrows, the song leader for the whole of the 50 years of Billy Graham's campaign ministry, was speaking to the National Fellowship of Church Musicians. I did not attend that conference, but I did read about the conference in *Decision* magazine and learned that Cliff had challenged several hundred worship and evangelical leaders in attendance, saying, "There's no contemporary hymnody being written." He went on to say, "I want to challenge you men and women to write hymns of this generation."

As a result, the National Fellowship of Church Musicians asked *Decision* magazine (which at that time had far wider circulation throughout the whole Body of Christ then it does now) to help sponsor a hymn-writing competition. When my mother found out about this, she called me and said, "Jack, if you will send in a hymn for this competition, you'll win." This publication reached the majority of the English-speaking world, but you know how most mothers are—they think their children are the greatest. She suggested I submit a hymn I had composed while at a conference in the Colorado Rockies. On that occasion I had been so deeply moved by the classic hymn "To God Be the Glory, Great Things He Has Done" that I was inspired to write something with a similar spirit and mood entitled "We Lift Our Voice Rejoicing."

To please Mamma, I sent it in. I discovered later that mine was one of 963 entries from around the world. The absolutely incredible thing was that Mamma had prophesied the truth—I won the hymn competition. This was the greatest thing that had happened in my life up to that time, and I was overwhelmed. My $100 in prize money would translate to about $500 dollars today.

I have continued to write hymns. For the Fourth of July, I wrote some special lyrics for our congregation to sing as an intercessory prayer for our nation to the tune of "America (My Country 'Tis of Thee)." The lyric began: "My country, 'tis for thee, I bow to intercede before my King." Our congregation was on their knees on Independence Day, singing that classic melody with a contemporary lyric that I had written for the occasion. I have also written lyrics with melodies, and I deeply believe in the need for the Church to continue to compose new hymns. In fact, Cliff Barrows's call of 1962 continues to resonate today: *We need to write hymns for this generation.*

WHAT MAY BE LACKING IN CONTEMPORARY WORSHIP SONGS

There are contemporary worship songs that inspire and move the individual but do not necessarily have words which were intended to teach, reach, enrich or edify a group of believers. I have no doubt that those who compose these songs were edified as the Holy Spirit gave these particular songs to them for their own private worship. However, a problem arises when any song is introduced to a congregation without the benefit of editing or reflection.

A song may have a nice melody and godly words and could have potential to be developed into something that would minister to people in a lasting and effective way. But if the song is not developed, it will tend to lack substance and therefore not really add anything to the depth and development of a congregation's understanding of the Lord. Unfortunately, some songs circulated within the larger Body of Christ lack this development and careful editing. These songs are not essentially bad lyrically, but they could say so much more.

In much of contemporary secular music there is a tendency toward mindless repetition that inhibits the capacity of the individual to think analytically and structurally. Sometimes the repeated phrase is so seductive and suggestive it's no wonder we have the teenage pregnancies we do. The pervading attitude of our culture is progressively and increasingly becoming anti-Christ; and the mindless repetition of contemporary music numbs people's minds and disables their thought processes, and eventually people fall prey to the ultimate deception and are manipulated by Satan.

The spirit of the world also seeks to distract and disable disciples of Jesus Christ. God is not against good feelings and entertainment, and this is not intended to be a diatribe against secular or popular Christian music. There will be songs that cause us to feel good, but the Church needs songs to take us further than the feel-goods; the Church needs songs that *disciple*.

> Do not be conformed to this world, but be transformed
> by the renewing of your mind (Rom. 12:2).

The renewing of our minds requires thought, and developing disciples are thinking people. Now, I am not advocating intellectualized worship. There are simple but profound songs that move me to my knees and allow me to express my feelings of love and affection for Jesus.

Much of Christian music today takes its cue from the culture of popular music and therefore reaches the world in the same dimension. While we need to be culturally relevant, we need to draw culture further than it arrives on its own. Christian music produced today is undoubtedly spiritual music with a spiritual message, but because much of it lacks lyrical depth and requires little thought from the listener, it is a poor discipleship tool. The music birthed from the hearts of believers can and should do so much more to strengthen the Church.

Again, I am not advocating a departure from popular, contemporary culture. Christian composers, lyricists and artists can incorporate some trends in popular music, but they should not entirely depend upon them. For example, the song "I Could Sing of Your Love Forever" by the British worship group Delirious incorporates repetition but does not depend upon it. I have been delighted to watch young people in our congregation sing this song, and it is obvious they are worshiping. I am happy because I know that they are being discipled by our youth pastors and that they have their minds on Jesus when they sing this song.

A FINAL WORD ON PARTICIPATION IN WORSHIP

Participation is key. We must be wary of allowing our congregations to simply enjoy the splendid music of gifted worship teams and not requiring corporate participation. A congregation of observers is definitely not the aim or goal of a worship service. As I mentioned at the outset, the worship leader leads the congregation before the throne of God and it takes sound leadership to bring the people to all God has for them. It is from this place that the Church will advance the kingdom of God in strength and power in the millennium set before us.

SHAKE DOWN THE THUNDER:
WORSHIP, WARFARE AND THE HARVEST

The following is adapted from an article by the author which first appeared in the September/October 1999 issue of Ministries Today *and is reprinted here by permission.*

A very unique sense of destiny is upon me these days. Perhaps you feel something of it, too. Because any thoughtful leader must sooner or later come to grips with this fact: *We are privileged to be Church leaders at what is unquestionably the most pivotal time in human history.* This isn't hyperbole—it's reality.

Around the world there is a global restlessness. As Jesus predicted, we are seeing an intense tide of nationalism—nation against nation (see Matt. 24:7)—sweeping the globe, bringing the "distress of nations, with perplexity" (Luke 21:25) to a crescendo. The cultural agenda is again being set by conflict but not at the superpower level. In lieu of the five decades of tortured peace the characterized the East-West standoff, we are now subjected to frighteningly unpredictable and politically unmanageable scenarios. At any moment, the world can expect to be victimized by the whimsy of a regional chieftain via a deadly act of terrorism. Any political cult, however bizarre, can disrupt an entire nation's equilibrium—and can purchase a nuclear device to destroy it. Even more terrifying is the fact that they don't need a stealth bomber to deliver it. A suitcase will do.

And yet sociologically there is a global sense of anticipation—an almost mystical sense of the approach of great hope (or great horror). I am amazed at the lengths to which people will go for a memorable or meaningful experience. Who can fathom millions of dollars that were spent as multitudes converged on "millennial sites"—from the top of the World Trade Center to the Great Wall of China—on December 31, 1999?

It is in this spiritual environment that we find the seeds of a vast global awakening. A century of worshiping the human intellect has ushered in an international famine, begetting a desperate quest for spiritual meaning. Having been on a society-wide forced diet rooted in the vain supposition that educational, scientific and technological advances can satisfy the hunger of the human soul, innumerable hosts, like confused sheep, are stampeding toward anything that offers the slightest promise of spiritual fulfillment.

At the same time, the Holy Spirit has been surging through the Church for an entire century—spreading revival and renewal while advancing *His* reformation. Not since the first century have the people of God been so ready to meet the challenge of reaching and feeding the multitudes. Equipped and ignited by the gifts and fire of the Holy Spirit and instructed in God's Word as never in history, millions within Christ's global Body are poised for an unprecedented harvest.

NO AUTOMATIC HARVEST

Clearly, the harvest beckons us. Yet for all our analysis and enthusiasm, we require a strategic sensitivity. Exuberant rhetoric declaring "The end times harvest is here!" can neither produce nor garner a single grain. This harvest will not be reaped through the simple pursuit of a golden opportunity. It will be realized only by employing God's strategy: The harvest will spring from living worship and be possessed by discerning warfare!

This call to strategic sensitivity vibrates within the deepest dimensions of my soul; I feel I am touching the pulse of God's heart as I write on the theme at hand. The Church must rise to stand in worship and in warfare if we are to move beyond expectancy. As in the words of Isaiah, the Church has been like a pregnant woman who has gone way beyond term but not given birth:

> As a woman with child . . . so have we been in Your sight, O LORD. We have been with child, we have been in pain; we have, as it were, brought forth wind; we have not accomplished any deliverance in the earth (Isa. 26:17,18).

In short, the opportunity was there, a travail was entered, but no real life has been birthed! If we continue on this path, we are far closer to experiencing fruitlessness in the new millennium than we are to reaping a harvest—unless we hear and heed a heavenly trumpet call.

Throwing Down a Gauntlet

To capture the unique spiritual opportunity before us at this millennial turning point, I am persuaded that the entire Body of Christ needs a spiritual shake-up and a shakedown. By a shake-up I mean to be *purged to the core* of our beings. Then we must "shake down the thunder," as in the classic lyric from the football fight song that proposes passion in pursuit—not business as usual.[1]

Recent observations compel me to cry out, not as anyone's judge or critic, but as a knight throwing down his gauntlet to challenge an offender of his regent's lady. In both areas of truth and practice—worship and warfare—I have witnessed the rise of a mocking spirit that seeks to compromise Jesus' Bride. Even as the Holy Spirit's purifying work is awakening worship in many quarters, there has risen a trend toward prioritizing sound over spirit, style over substance, performance over participation and personnel over power.

This disturbing trend is changing the definition of what our people call worship. More and more we are hearing "worship" defined as the *music presented* by a group and its leader, rather than as an *entrance* into the throne room of God by a congregation. Foot-tapping giddiness and warm, fuzzy feelings is not worship; life-transforming joy and abject humility in God's presence is.

If you are a pastor or worship leader, your leadership mandate is for long-term results, not short-term sensation or excitement. No matter how nifty worship looks in my church, I must remain sensitive as to whether my congregation's worship habits are manifesting in a momentary buzz of excitement or an "eternal weight of glory" (2 Cor. 4:17).

The same goes for "spiritual warfare"—a phrase that has become both scorned and elitist amid increased discussion of prayer, fasting and intercession. Scorn is leveled by theological critics who judge the subject of spiritual warfare as a province of the ignorantly excitable who have missed the deeper meaning of Christ's conclusive triumph. On the other hand, elitism distills in some circles where there is displayed an air of mystery and condescension toward those segments of the Church that are apparently less insightful.

But the Lord is calling us to lead the way toward the "simplicity that is in Christ" (2 Cor. 11:3) with regard to worship and warfare. What we do or do not do in the coming years will determine whether the harvest is to be watered and reaped—being conceived in worship and possessed through warfare—or to be left to whither and die.

PERFECTING PRAISE

Three decades of leadership in the arenas of worship and warfare have taught me one thing: There are no accomplished experts. I am persuaded that all our experience in worship and warfare means little; I can never gain seniority in either field, for I am called to enter both exercises as a child—every time!

Out of the mouths of babes and infants you have ordained strength, because of Your enemies, that You may silence the enemy (Ps. 8:2).

Jesus describes this childlike worship as "perfected praise" (Matt. 21:16).

Those who are willing to become as babes are the ones who will realize the harvest—not by their might or power, their style or sophistication, their insights or discernment. Just as the Lord of the harvest has called us to lift up our eyes and see the fields of opportunity (see John 4:35), so the Lord of glory is calling us to "lift our hearts" in worshipful humility (Lam. 3:41) and to lift up our hands in prayerful intercession unto evangelism's breakthrough (see 1 Tim. 2:8).

As a leader, there is a passion and a pattern I dare never presume I've mastered.

ENDNOTES

Chapter 2

1. Revelation 12:9 tells us that Satan, the serpent and the dragon are one and the same. Jesus not only treated the devil as a personal being and acknowledged his temporary claim to power on this planet (see Matt. 4:1-10), but He also spoke of Adam and Eve as being actual people (see Matt. 19:4,5). Both facts remove the matter of evil's source and man's beginning and purpose from the realm of mythology or speculation.

Chapter 7

1. The Lord repeatedly emphasized that the priests' ministry was to serve Him (see Exod. 28:1, 3,4,41; 29:1,44; 30:30; 40:13,15).
2. Ezekiel 40—48 elaborates details of this Temple's construction and ministry.

Chapter 9

1. The death of Eli's sons at this same time probably caused the absence of an adult in the role of high priest, which was a hereditary position.
2. Compare 1 Chronicles 16:7-36 with Psalms 96:1-13; 105:1-15 and 106:1,47,48.

Chapter 10

1. See Luke 24:50; Acts 2:46,47; 4:24; 20:36; 1 Corinthians 14:15; 16:1-3; 1 Timothy 2:8; 2 Timothy 2:15.

2. Author's paraphrase of Romans 12:1,2. The joining of "intelligent" and "spiritual" is consistent with the dual components contained in the Greek words *logiken latre ian.*

Chapter 12

1. *The Open Bible, Expanded Edition,* notes on 1 Chronicles 29:4,7.

Appendix 4

1. The lyric is from the fabled "Notre Dame Victory March." Written by two brothers, Irish alumni Michael J. Shea and John F. Shea, the song debuted in 1908, when Michael played it on the organ of the Second Congregational Church in Holyoke, Massachusetts. The lyrics begin "Cheer, cheer for old Notre Dame. Wake up the echoes cheering her name. Send the volley cheer on high. Shake down the thunder from the sky."

REGAL BOOKS BY
JACK HAYFORD

Built by the Spirit

The Christmas Miracle

The Heart of Praise

I'll Hold You in Heaven

Loving Your City into the Kingdom
(with Ted Haggard)

Pastors of Promise

To contact the author or for more information about Living Way Ministries or about The King's College and Seminary, call or write:

Living Way Ministries
14820 Sherman Way
Van Nuys, CA 91405-2233
Phone: (800) 776-8180
www.livingway.org
www.kingsseminary.edu

Best-Sellers from Regal

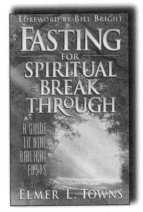

A Guide to Nine Biblical Fasts
Elmer Towns
Paperback
ISBN 08307.18397

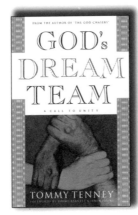

A Call to Unity
Tommy Tenney
Paperback
ISBN 08307.23846

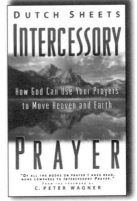

How God Can Use Your Prayers
to Move Heaven and Earth
Dutch Sheets
Paperback
ISBN 08307.19008

Daily Devotions for Drawing
Near to God and One Another
Dennis and Barbara Rainey
Hardcover
ISBN 08307.17544

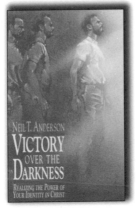

Realizing the Power of
Your Identity in Christ
Neil T. Anderson
Paperback
ISBN 08307.25644

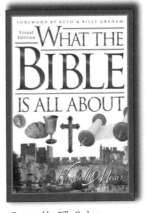

Foreword by Billy Graham
Henrietta Mears
Visual Edition
ISBN 08307.24311
Also available in KJV and NIV editions

Best-Sellers from Regal

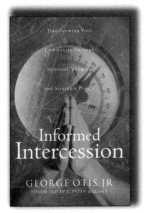
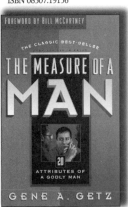
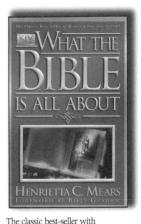